Making the Case for
PROFESSIONAL SERVICE

by ERNEST A. LYNTON

Published in collaboration with
New England Resource Center for Higher Education
University of Massachusetts at Boston

STERLING, VIRGINIA

Originally published by AAHE

THE AUTHOR

Ernest Lynton has long and consistently advocated for greater attention to professional service. As early as 1983, in a *Change* magazine article "A Crisis of Purpose: Reexamining the Role of the University," he called for "faster and more effective dissemination of information and research to potential users." With coauthor Sandra Elman, he elaborated on the topic in *New Priorities for the University: Meeting Society's Needs for Applied Knowledge and Competent Individuals* (Jossey-Bass, 1987). He has since written and spoken extensively on professional service and related topics. Recently, he worked with Ernest Boyer on *Scholarship Assessed*, the Carnegie Foundation's follow-up report to its best-selling *Scholarship Reconsidered*.

Lynton is Commonwealth Professor and senior associate of the New England Resource Center for Higher Education of the University of Massachusetts at Boston. He began his professional career as a physicist, working at Rutgers from 1952 until 1973, first as a faculty member and then as founding dean of its Livingston College. He served as senior vice president for academic affairs for the University of Massachusetts system from 1973 until 1980.

His work on this monograph was supported by the Carnegie Foundation for the Advancement of Teaching.

MAKING THE CASE FOR PROFESSIONAL SERVICE
by Ernest A. Lynton
Copyright © 1995 by the American Association for Higher Education. Copyright © 2005 by Stylus Publishing, LLC. All rights reserved. Printed in the United States of America.

The materials reproduced in the Appendix appear with the permission of their publishers.

For information about additional copies of this publication or other AAHE or Stylus publications, contact:
Stylus Publishing, LLC
22883 Quicksilver Drive
Sterling, VA 20166-2102
Tel.: 1-800-232-0223 / Fax: 703-661-1547
www.Styluspub.com

ISBN 1-56377-033-4

Contents

FOREWORD

by Russell Edgerton
President, American Association for Higher Education

In the early 1990s, when faculty priorities and the university reward system surfaced as a major item on the higher education agenda, AAHE established a new program, the Forum on Faculty Roles & Rewards, to help campuses work through the issues. With a generous grant from the Fund for the Improvement of Postsecondary Education, we have sponsored an annual national conference, provided an ongoing clearinghouse, and initiated investigations of key issues. This monograph is the fruit of one of these particular investigations.

When we first began the Forum, the most pressing issue universities faced was how to adjust workloads and the reward systems to meet the insistent public demand that faculty pay more attention to undergraduate teaching. But as we began to work through these issues of the status of teaching, we became aware that lurking behind them was another concern: that providing service to the larger community be elevated in status, as well.

We also knew that venturing into this area of university activity would take us quickly onto soft and mushy ground. The territory itself — what *community* means, and what "needs" are there to serve — is vast and ill-defined. The argument for faculty to provide professional service turns less on the need to respond to insistent "demands" than on the more general benefits of becoming more central to the life of the larger society . . . a tougher case to make.

But wait, it gets worse. Within the university, professional outreach has traditionally been confused with obligations of institutional citizenship to the university. And to complicate matters further, professional outreach doesn't occur in standardized units that lend themselves easily to evaluation. While faculty teaching unfolds in the context of standardized units we call courses, faculty service takes the form of ad hoc projects and ongoing relationships, where the beginnings and endings and intended beneficiaries of the service being provided are often much harder to define.

All this is to say that when Clara Lovett and Ernest Lynton first proposed to mount an expedition into this terrain, I secretly admired their courage but feared they might never return. Knowing how little each had in way of time or resources to devote to the project added to my concern. And when Clara Lovett became president of Northern

Arizona University midway into the project, I resigned myself to the fact that if I ever saw our good colleague Ernest Lynton again it would certainly not be with a manuscript in hand. But lo and behold, he did return, and *with* a manuscript. Gene Rice, current director of the Forum, joins me in saying thanks to Clara Lovett for initiating this project and special thanks to Ernest Lynton for seeing it through.

Making the Case for Professional Service I view as a new map of the terrain, supplementing and taking us beyond the very useful guide, *Professional Service and Faculty Rewards,* that Sandra Elman and Sue Smock authored in 1985. Ernie takes on professional outreach at several levels, so there is grist and guidance here — both for campus leaders who make policy as well as for individual faculty who do outreach and who seek and deserve more recognition for this work. His central thesis — that the key to elevating the status of professional service is to capture the "scholarship" of professional service for review by peers — is also central to the work the Forum is doing in teaching, and one we wholeheartedly endorse.

There is much work yet to be done in this area. We don't imagine this monograph to be the last word. Rather, we hope it will act as a catalyst — as AAHE's 1991 *The Teaching Portfolio* did for teaching — for creating a campus culture in which the value of professional service both to the institution and to society is recognized, and faculty are properly rewarded for undertaking it. □

ACKNOWLEDGEMENTS

This volume is based on the effort of many individuals. Clara Lovett, former director of the AAHE Forum on Faculty Roles & Rewards, helped to define the task and played a central role in its evolution over time, continuing to do so even after assuming the arduous presidency of Northern Arizona University. She, as well as Nevin Brown, a principal partner of AAHE's Education Trust, interviewed individual faculty members on several campuses engaged in professional service and gathered useful information. Russ Edgerton, president of AAHE, did much to improve both the initial conception of the monograph and its successive drafts by giving me the benefit of his critical but supportive analysis and his incisive comments. He also came up with its title, which with one phrase reflects the dual purpose of this volume.

I also benefitted a great deal from the advice provided by Dr. Lovett's successor, Gene Rice, since he took over the direction of the Forum. Project assistant Kris Sorchy most ably, and graciously, assisted with the many logistical details. And once the manuscript reached its final form, Bry Pollack, director of publications at AAHE, provided her invaluable editorial and publishing skills.

In the early stages of the Forum's work on professional service, an ad hoc group of faculty and administrators from a number of universities and colleges, as well as some representatives of professional associations, came together several times at the AAHE offices to help shape the monograph's outline and direction. Also contributing much were all those individual faculty members on a number of campuses who willingly and patiently submitted themselves to lengthy interviews by Clara Lovett, Nevin Brown, or myself. Special thanks are due to those who agreed to allow publication of abbreviated case descriptions based on their actual work. They are, in alphabetical order, Howard Cohen, now interim provost and professor of philosophy at the University of Wisconsin, Parkside; Michael Cummings, professor of geology at Portland State University; Peter Kiang, associate professor of education at the University of Massachusetts at Boston; Allan Myerson, dean of the School of Chemical and Material Science and professor of chemical engineering at New York Polytechnic University; and Noel Stowe, professor of history and acting dean of the graduate school at Arizona State University. Howard Cohen and Noel Stowe provided helpful comments, as well, on the manuscript as a whole.

I'm also grateful to have been given permission by Michigan State University, the University of North Carolina at Chapel Hill, and the University of Illinois at Urbana-

Champaign to reproduce pertinent documents provided by them in the APPENDIX.

It should be clear from these acknowledgements that the monograph represents truly a collective effort, and that I functioned in substantial measure as a compiler and editor of the work of others. All those I've mentioned contributed substantially to what merit the monograph has. None is responsible for its remaining shortcomings.

This is most particularly the case with regard to Ernest Boyer, president of the Carnegie Foundation for the Advancement of Teaching, who played an important role in the evolution of this monograph, both by supporting my work financially and also by adding substantially to my understanding of the nature of scholarship, its documentation, and the measures of its quality. In 1991, he asked me to generate background material and an initial draft for a follow-up report to *Scholarship Reconsidered.* That assignment provided me with a unique opportunity not only to sharpen and enlarge ideas I had suggested in prior publications about the nature of the scholarly process, but also to profit from a number of intensive discussions with Dr. Boyer as well as Dr. Mary Huber, director of policy studies at the Foundation, which substantially enriched and shaped my conceptions of scholarship. This monograph benefitted greatly from those discussions and reflects the insights that these two colleagues helped me to achieve.

ERNEST A. LYNTON
Brookline, MA
January 1995

MAKING THE CASE FOR "MAKING THE CASE"

This is a monograph about institutional outreach by means of faculty **professional service** — that is, work by faculty members based on their scholarly expertise and contributing to the mission of the institution. Through outreach a university or a college becomes a direct intellectual resource for its external constituencies.

I have long been interested in this topic, worried that the substantial neglect of institutional outreach has created a widening gap between society's external expectations for higher education and our internal priorities. Back in 1983, in an article in *Change* called "A Crisis of Purpose: Reexamining the Role of the University," I wrote that

> *Acceleration of change requires faster and more effective dissemination of information and research to potential users — industry, governmental and legislative agencies, public and private sector bodies, and the public at large. Ours is a knowledge-intensive society, and there is enormous and growing need not only for data but even more for analysis and synthesis, for explication, technical assistance, and public information. . . . [I]t is the increasing responsibility of the university not merely to be a principal source of new knowledge but also to be instrumental in analyzing and applying this knowledge and in making it rapidly useful to all societal sectors* (pp. 23, 53).

Because that responsibility must, of necessity, be carried out by members of the faculty, I added that their involvement in this outreach should be recognized "as parts of a broad spectrum of important scholarly activity" (p. 53).

In a subsequent book, *New Priorities for the University*, coauthored with Sandra Elman, I elaborated on the theme in considerable detail (Lynton and Elman, 1987), as have I in a number of articles since then. Elman and Smock added an important element to these earlier discussions of professional service with their NASULGC report, *Professional Service and Faculty Rewards: Toward an Integrated Structure* (1985).

Today there is ever greater urgency for higher education to change its priorities. External demands for outreach have multiplied, the public trust in higher education has diminished, and competition for public and private funds has increased. In such a context, academic institutions must reassess their external obligations. At the same time, ever more insistent questions are being raised about the nature of the education we provide. The seminal work of Donald Schön (1983) together with widespread employer dissatisfaction with our graduates force us to take a new look at the relationship of theory to practice in our teaching.

These external pressures have acted to intensify a national debate about faculty work and the nature of scholarship that began with the publication of Ernest Boyer's *Scholarship Reconsidered* (1990) and has been carried forward by the AAHE Forum on Faculty Roles & Rewards. In that debate, a much needed focus on teaching must now be supplemented by attention, as well, to professional service. The time has come for action in this area, not just talk about the need for it. We must move beyond the exhortations of the past and focus on implementation.

THE PURPOSES OF THIS MONOGRAPH

It is my hope that this monograph will contribute in concrete ways to restoring professional service to the important role it once had in American higher education, and to encouraging that it be carried out at high levels of quality and be rewarded accordingly. The monograph is intended to be a working document that can be used by a university or college, by departments and other units within an institution, and by individual faculty members as each attempts to translate broad principles into terms, policies, and procedures applicable to specific circumstances.

Its first part focuses on making the case at every institutional level for a substantially greater emphasis on professional service. General arguments are supplemented by detailed discussions of the nature of professional service and illustrated by five short case descriptions. The combination should enable individual departments and other such units to begin the discussion of what professional service means in terms specific to their discipline or field and to their circumstances. A set of questions with which a department can get started on this exploration is included.

Another purpose of the monograph is to assist individual faculty members engaged in professional service in making the case for the quality of their work, and also to help those charged with the review of such work to evaluate it. Accordingly, the second part of the monograph describes how a faculty member can demonstrate the scholarly nature of a professional service project, using the abbreviated case studies as examples. It discusses the principal elements needed to document the work, identifies potential sources of evidence, and suggests criteria by which the quality of the work can be assessed. Such documentation is intended to provide a rich description of the faculty member's work — not only for promotion and tenure and other formal rewards but also as a formative tool in collegial discussions about professional service.

With regard to both kinds of "making the case," this monograph stops short of being a detailed how-to manual, with specific directions for each field. Instead, it aims to provide sufficient illustrative material, as well as actual questions to be pursued, so as to trigger and inform the discipline-specific discussion that must take place, department by department and unit by unit, before genuine change can occur on a campus. Only by means of such campus-wide discourse can a university or college create an institutional culture in which professional service is recognized as a collective obligation and taken seriously — in performance, in collegial discourse, and in formal evaluation and reward. The monograph, I hope, will serve as a catalyst for creating such a culture, and it ends with an Action Agenda for that purpose.   □

A RENEWED NEED FOR AN OLD TRADITION

I n recent years, the call for academic institutions to be more responsive to societal needs has become ever more urgent, and has now been taken up by many influential voices in higher education. In a recent issue of *The Chronicle of Higher Education*, Ernest Boyer writes about the "New American College":

> *Higher education and the larger purposes of American society are inextricably intertwined. . . . A commitment to service as well as teaching and research was never more needed than now. . . . Higher education has more intellectual talent than any other institution in our culture. Today's colleges and universities surely must respond to the challenges that confront society* (1994).

That response must of course include, in greater measure than ever before, basic and applied research to enhance the overall capability of higher education to meet the challenges to which Boyer refers. Colleges and universities must continue to strive to discover, to innovate, and to understand better the social and economic forces shaping our world.

But discovery is not enough. As Allan Bromley, distinguished nuclear physicist and science advisor to President Reagan, pointed out about science back in 1982, challenges face us on both internal and external frontiers. The internal frontiers are "those boundaries where human knowledge is pushing most vigorously toward the unknown"; the external frontiers, characterized by Bromley as "no less important" than the internal, are those that border application (Bromley, 1982). *Both* frontiers demand the attention of higher education.

What is true for science is true for other fields of inquiry, especially in view of the growing complexity and seeming intractability of contemporary society's problems. The crisis of our schools, the condition of our cities, the growing gap between rich and poor: These are among what William Greiner, president of SUNY Buffalo, has called "a chaos of cries for help, understanding, new frameworks and ideas and solutions" (1994, p. 12).

The challenge of societal needs cannot be met by higher education alone. But colleges and universities have a special responsibility as institutions solely dedicated to the advancement of knowledge. The cries to which Greiner refers are for

> *things that universities, by nature and inclination, are good at producing . . . [they] are as well equipped and more obligated than virtually any other social institution to listen, understand, and respond to the desperate voices of our people* (p. 12).

Colleges and universities — especially but not only those that receive public support — have an inescapable responsibility to play a central role. And that responsibility is particularly great toward those elements in society that lack the capability themselves to keep up with the rapid evolution of the knowledge they need to cope with their tasks. Of the great deal that is known about societal issues, too little is actually used in the development of policies and their implementation. As one state official recently told an academic group: "There are plenty of ideas about what to do: Help us to apply them."

Knowledge is not an inert commodity to be stored like the gold in Fort Knox.

The small manufacturing company, unable to afford its own R&D, needs help to keep up-to-date technologically. Schools are looking for collaboration in curriculum revision, personnel development, and management. Government, both legislative and executive, needs not only. access to information but also help in aggregating and interpreting what information is available — a need felt as strongly by community and other nonprofit groups. Others need policy analysis and program evaluation, or organizational and personnel development. And society generally has a critical need for more and better public information.

This myriad of needs is why so many voices are urging American higher education to revive its tradition of service and to restore the centrality of that service to institutional missions. What's required is a renewed commitment within the academy to direct outreach to society. As former president Charles McCallum of the University of Alabama at Birmingham stated recently:

> [W]e must change the pervasive faculty idea that a university's activities can
> be executed without regard to the needs of the surrounding community (1994,
> p. 16).

The time between the development of an idea and its potential application has been extraordinarily shortened (Adamany, 1983). No longer can colleges and universities wait passively for new information to disseminate via their traditional, "trickle down" mode of scholarly publication. Instead, academic institutions, through the work of their faculties, must become active agents in ensuring that new knowledge quickly and effectively reaches those who need it.

> While continuing to devote themselves to the ongoing creation of new knowledge,
> [faculty] increasingly need to apply both their resources and their expertise to

other components of the complex process through which knowledge is absorbed by society (Lynton and Elman, 1987, p. 2).

THE NATURE OF KNOWLEDGE

Turning to other parts of this process is potentially as exciting and creative as it is important. Knowledge is not an inert commodity to be stored like the gold in Fort Knox, or dispensed like a patent medicine. If that were the case, then the dissemination and application of new ideas and techniques could be left to technicians and technology.

Knowledge is different. It is dynamic, constantly made fresh and given new shape by its interaction with reality. Its application constitutes learning for the scholar, arising out of his or her reflection on the situation-specific aspects of the act of application. No two school systems, no two businesses, no two government agencies, no two community groups are identical. While the problems they face may share some basic elements, when the specific situation of each is illuminated in the light of pertinent theories and principles, it displays special features that call for an innovative and creative response tailored to its unique circumstances. In turn, what the scholar learns from the specific instance feeds back into a better general understanding of the issues in question.

Because the application of knowledge is so highly situation-specific, it is a task that must be carried out case by case, and thus undertaken throughout higher education. Opportunities and challenges abound for community and liberal arts colleges, for comprehensive and research universities. Daunting societal issues exist at national and indeed global levels, and some institutions will focus on these. Other institutions will concentrate on local and regional problems of comparable complexity. Each university and college can contribute in its own fashion.

Progress along this line will benefit our knowledge-hungry society (and improve the quality of teaching, learning, and research within the institution, as will be discussed presently). In so doing, such progress may help to restore public confidence in higher education, countering the widespread perception that academic institutions, most particularly the universities, are disconnected from the concerns and needs of society.

Our external publics probably are too narrowly focused on immediate responses and short-term impact, little understanding the continuing need for long-term, curiosity-driven inquiry; however, to explain and justify the importance of that inquiry, higher education must work harder to assure that the knowledge it already has gets applied. As Greiner put it:

> *There is still an enormous reservoir of trust and hope [among the public] regarding universities and colleges, a reservoir that can be tapped if we but show that we care about and are willing to engage in the resolution of pressing social needs* (1994, p. 14).

RESTORING A PROUD TRADITION

Leaders of American higher education a century ago would have wholeheartedly endorsed a renewed emphasis on professional service. Our historically strong commitment to outreach strikingly distinguishes higher education in the United States from that in other countries. As a well-known British observer of American higher education once remarked, "the great American contribution to higher education has been to dismantle the walls around the campus" (Ashby, 1967, p. 4).

The commitment to service, characteristic of American higher education from its very beginning *(cf.,* e.g., Ehrlich, 1995), was much strengthened in the state universities by the Morrill Land-Grant Act of 1862. It found its full expression toward the turn of the century, with the passage of the Hatch and the Smith-Lever Acts establishing agricultural experiment stations and the cooperative extension system, and the pronouncement of the "Wisconsin Idea" by President Van Hise of the University of Wisconsin, which rested on "the conviction that informed intelligence when applied to the problems of modern society could make democracy work more effectively" (Rudolph, 1962, p. 363).

"Service" then had a very precise meaning. It signified **the utilization of a university as an intellectual resource for its immediate as well as broader constituencies**. It implied a **collective responsibility** integral and important to the institutional mission. When Van Hise proclaimed that the boundaries of his university were the boundaries of the state, he meant not only that the institution would be open to students from all parts of the state but also that it would provide professional expertise to public agencies and private enterprises throughout Wisconsin.

Of course, the outreach mission of an institution embodied in the "Wisconsin Idea" could be carried out only through the work of its faculty and staff. Hence, institutional commitment to service in turn meant recognition of service as an important faculty activity. Service as an individual activity was understood to be the **application of the individual's professional expertise to problems and tasks outside the campus**. It did not mean committee work on campus, nor work for professional or disciplinary associations; it did not mean collecting for the United Way or jury duty, however important and worthwhile all of these activities might have been then and continue to be now.

Sadly, over the years, and especially in the decades following World War II, the term "service" has increasingly taken on these other meanings of good institutional, disciplinary, and general citizenship. Institutional as well as individual faculty commitment to outreach diminished as "service" came to denote good deeds rather than creative intellectual effort. And, as a result, service is now a very distant third, behind research and teaching, in institutional attention and incentives.

Now American higher education is being urged from many sides to change that situation. It is being exhorted to turn the rhetoric of mission statements into the reality of an **institutional commitment** to direct interaction with public and private-sector constituencies, helping them to apply the latest knowledge and the latest techniques to the analysis and amelioration of their problems. And higher education must respond — but respond properly: by recognizing this kind of service as an integral component of its collective mission, and not leave it to individual faculty initiative.   □

INSTITUTIONAL BENEFITS

Professional service not only benefits society. In a variety of ways it contributes substantially to the quality and intellectual vitality of a college or university.

First, as described earlier, if properly carried out, professional service treats knowledge as a dynamic and exciting entity, not an inert commodity. It is not a one-way flow of information and technical assistance to external clients; instead, it is a two-way communication that provides substantial opportunities for discovery and fresh insights. Each of the five professional service projects described later in this monograph (see MAKING THE CASE) illustrates this. As Derek Bok, former president of Harvard, pointed out more than a decade ago in *Beyond the Ivory Tower*:

> *Efforts to understand economic and social development require a constant interaction between experience in the field and attempts to construct useful concepts and theories* (1982).

A recent campus report, *University Outreach at Michigan State University* (excerpted in APPENDIX 1), makes a similar point this way:

> *Outreach affords . . . windows on current reality, and the perspectives gained through these windows inform a scholar's understanding of the contemporary meaning, value, and use of their disciplinary or professional knowledge. Outreach also raises fascinating and important questions. As a result, on-campus research and teaching become more vital, more alive, and the intellectual life of the whole university is more stimulating.*

Research in a practice context has become an essential contributor to progress in the social sciences, in humanistic fields such as ethics, and in many technical and scientific fields, as well. Professional service provides a bridge between practice and theory, and thereby can enhance the knowledge base of academic disciplines and professional fields. Professional service helps to test the validity of basic paradigms and identifies new targets of inquiry. As a "Statement on the Professional Work of Faculty in Geography," issued in 1994 by the Association of American Geographers, states:

> *For faculty to undertake outreach would yield worthwhile dividends, including . . . [a]ugmented theoretical development engendered by the propensity of the world to work contrary to theory-based expectations [and] enhanced faculty proficiency in both teaching and research as a result of grappling with substantive problems* (see Diamond and Adam, eds.).

Thus, professional service can itself become a source of innovation and discovery in both theory and methodology. The case study projects in public history, ethics, and engineering, for example, each contributes both to its discipline and to the methodology of outreach; the geology and education cases are innovative with regard to methodology (see MAKING THE CASE).

Professional service helps to test the validity of basic paradigms, and identifies new targets of inquiry.

Second, professional service is of great importance — in some ways even *essential* — to the quality of instruction in colleges and universities, especially but not only in professional education. The influential work of Donald Schön on the nature of professional practice as "reflection-in-action" (1983) has raised serious questions about how future practitioners can best be prepared for their work (Schön, 1987; Curry et al., 1993). These questions are receiving increasing attention on many campuses and from a number of professional associations.

Traditional professional curricula are based on an implicit hierarchy in which applied science is derived from basic science and in turn yields "diagnostic and problem-solving techniques which are applied . . . to the actual delivery of services" (Schön, 1983, p. 24). In this traditional approach, clinical components of the curriculum serve merely to develop skills in the use of theory and technique. Schön and others challenge this view, believing instead that "in many applied fields, knowledge emerges from the complexity and rigors of practice" (Rice and Richlin, 1993, p. 287). That belief changes the role and timing of clinical practice in professional education in fundamental ways, eliminating the prevalent separation of theory from practice. It leads to the recognition that

(1) education for the professions, at every level, should be organized to a greater extent around the problems of practice; (2) . . . provide opportunities for reflection-in-action and reflection-about-action among novices and experts; and (3) evaluation of students and practicing professionals must include . . . assessment of performance in the complex situations of practice (Harris, 1993, pp. 51-52; *cf.* also Cavanaugh, 1993).

To date, little attention has been paid to the profound implications this new perspective on professional education has for all faculty charged with the education of future practitioners, whether or not those faculty are directly involved in practical components of the curriculum. One obvious implication is that they must themselves understand at firsthand the relationship of their discipline to the complexity of actual situations in which it is applied. No better way exists for faculty to do so than to be themselves engaged in professional service. In addition, faculty involvement in professional service also provides students with opportunities to participate as assistants or in independent projects.

The pedagogic importance of faculty professional service is not limited to the education of practitioners. Lee Shulman has recommended that we think about what he terms "public and community service" as a "clinical component for the liberal arts and sciences" (1991, p. 1). The ethics and the geology projects described in the case studies later in this monograph are two good examples of the engagement of liberal arts students in professional service. They show that such involvement constitutes an excellent opportunity for what has come to be called "service-learning." The growing interest in such activity reflects acceptance of the famous statement of Alfred North Whitehead that "education is the acquisition of the art of the utilization of knowledge." If students — especially at the undergraduate level — are not only to learn the content of the disciplines but to become aware, as well, of how the disciplines are applied in actual practice, then it is essential that the faculty themselves be knowledgeable about the "utilization" of what they teach. What better way to accomplish this than for faculty in all disciplines to be engaged in scholarly professional service, and for students to participate with them. (We will return to service-learning in a moment.)

To these quite tangible institutional benefits of professional service it is possible to add one other. As stated in that Michigan State report:

Outreach, when viewed as a scholarly activity, represents an exciting and attractive opportunity for faculty (see **APPENDIX 1**).

In responding to life-cycle issues (e.g., Knefelkamp, 1990) in faculty careers, and the importance of legitimating as valuable and valued a greater range of faculty activities, attention should turn toward professional service. To engage in applications of their expertise can prove invigorating and intellectually revivifying for many members of the faculty.

INDICATORS OF CHANGE

Straws are in the wind that this decade will witness significant progress in restoring professional service to a more central role in higher education.

One is the growing number of pertinent statements such as those quoted in this monograph, by university presidents, by heads of national higher education associations, and by other influential figures such as Ernest Boyer. Rhetoric alone is not enough, but it does gradually affect attitudes and shape the nature of the discourse.

Promising as well is a rapidly expanding interest and involvement by institutions in encouraging students to perform community service, and in transforming that service into a significant learning experience. Initially, the movement, usually called service-learning, remained quite separate from issues of faculty work and the nature of scholarship. More recently, however, the evident relationship between service-learning and faculty involvement in professional service is receiving attention. The two developments are beginning to overlap and to reinforce each other. The Michigan State University report on outreach, for example, explicitly recommends that

> *Involving students . . . in outreach should be a distinguishing feature of the Michigan State University educational experience* (see APPENDIX 1).

Ira Harkavy, of the University of Pennsylvania, calls for "problem-driven, problem-solving, real-world focused service-learning that integrates research and teaching with service" in a recent publication of Campus Compact, a national organization dedicated to integrating student service with academic learning (1993, p. 122). The same Campus Compact publication cites interesting examples of student involvement in faculty-directed service projects at Vanderbilt and Cornell Universities (p. 150).

A third indicator of change is that a growing number of comprehensive universities in urban and metropolitan regions have declared themselves to be "interactive universities," committed to being major intellectual resources to their regional constituencies in both the public and the private sectors. The group includes widely visible institutions such as the University of Illinois at Chicago and the University of Alabama at Birmingham. The group has formed a Coalition of Urban and Metropolitan Universities, which organizes biannual national meetings and sponsors a quarterly journal, *Metropolitan Universities.*

Much other evidence exists, as well. As part of a major initiative by Robert Diamond and his colleagues at Syracuse University, supported by Lilly Endowment Inc., a number of disciplinary and professional associations have drafted statements that address how their fields define scholarship, with particular attention to modes of professional service. Statements from several of these associations are collected in a publication soon to be published by AAHE (see Diamond and Adam, eds.). They are interesting both in their differences in detail and in their similarities in basic principle, and provide an excellent starting point for a department's or professional school's discussion of professional service.

With substantial support from the Kellogg Foundation, Michigan State University is examining the multidimensional tasks of a modern state university, with considerable emphasis on restoring to a more central position the traditional extension or outreach function. The project has included other members of the Big Ten Midwestern universities in addition to MSU. MSU also currently is developing a collaborative project with four other prominent state universities: Clemson, Oregon State, and the Universities of Minnesota-Twin Cities and Wisconsin-Madison. The stated purpose of the undertaking is well expressed in the title of its grant application: "Beyond Rhetoric to Action: Realigning Universities to Better Serve Society" (Votruba, 1994).

The collaborating publisher of this monograph, the New England Resource Center for Higher Education, at the University of Massachusetts at Boston, has initiated a major project to encourage community-oriented service by colleges and universities in New England. It will collect and disseminate pertinent materials, provide workshops and consultancies, and develop a regional network for the exchange of information and ideas. The project aims to become a prototype for similar efforts in other regions.

The most significant development in recent years was the publication of Ernest Boyer's *Scholarship Reconsidered,* and the widespread response it received. This 1990 report of the Carnegie Foundation for the Advancement of Teaching called for a broader conception of scholarship, to include not only traditional research but also teaching and professional service as valued dimensions of faculty work. Subsequently, AAHE received support from the Fund for the Improvement of Postsecondary Education to launch the Forum on Faculty Roles & Rewards, of which this monograph is a product. A large number of colleges and universities now are reviewing and adapting their policies in the area of faculty roles and rewards; while the emphasis to date has been mostly on the documentation, evaluation, and incentives for teaching, increasing attention is beginning to be paid to professional outreach, as well.

> **Professional service must be able to call on a significant part of the institution's human and material resources.**

SUPPORTING INSTITUTIONAL COMMITMENT TO PROFESSIONAL SERVICE

If professional service is to become an important part of the responsibilities of a college or university, it cannot remain at the margins, squeezed in as an uncompensated overload either for the institution as a whole or for any individual faculty member engaged in such service.

As an institutional priority, professional service must be able to call on a significant part of the institution's human and material resources and must, therefore, be explicitly factored into that institution's long- and short-range planning, as well as into its resource allocation processes. Appropriate external support must, in general, be made available explicitly — as part of the institutional operating budget, as part of an institutional or individual faculty grant or contract, or as institutional or individual fees for service. Given its proper importance, professional service is not a philanthropic activity.

Of course, institutions, especially public ones, frequently make political decisions to provide some professional service *pro bono*. But *pro bono* does not mean it costs nothing. Instead, it means that, like instruction and unfunded research, such service is funded by the regular appropriation or other support of the institution — that is, recognized as making demands on institutional resources. If these resources are limited, then an institution's commitment to *pro bono* service might mean its having to make difficult choices and perhaps cut back on other institutional activities to achieve its professional service goal.

Under no circumstance should the burden of an institution's decision to swallow the real cost of substantial outreach activities be placed on the shoulders of its faculty. Professional service by a faculty member must be carried out either as part of the workload in lieu of other assignments or, within the usual limits, as compensated overload funded from internal or external sources. In this way, an institution indicates its recognition of the legitimacy and importance of professional service as proper scholarly activity.

Viewing professional service as an **institutional priority** is important because only when it is recognized as a priority will professional service as an **individual faculty activity** be given the serious attention and the proper incentives it requires and deserves. As the Michigan State report declares:

> *Valuing and rewarding faculty participation represent the centerpiece for university outreach* (see **APPENDIX 1**).

We'll return to this key point in a later section.   □

WHAT IS PROFESSIONAL SERVICE?

I t is appropriate at this stage to take a closer look at the meaning of the term **professional service**. There is growing consensus throughout higher education that, as first suggested by Elman and Smock in their 1985 report *Professional Service and Faculty Rewards,* professional service is **work based on the faculty member's professional expertise that contributes to the mission of the institution.**

The Elman-Smock definition of professional service has been elaborated on by a number of statements from disciplinary and professional associations (see Diamond and Adam, eds.) and by many campuses. For example, in a 1993 policy statement (reproduced in APPENDIX 4), the University of Illinois at Urbana-Champaign describes professional service activities this way:

▶ *They contribute to the public welfare or the common good.*

▶ *They call upon faculty members' academic and/or professional expertise.*

▶ *They directly address or respond to real-world problems, issues, interests or concerns.*

A very similar definition has been proposed at the University of North Carolina at Chapel Hill (see APPENDIX 2 and 3) and at several other major state universities.

To clarify the concept of professional service, it is useful to consider some of the many forms it can take:

— technology transfer   — community development
— technical assistance   — program development
— policy analysis   — professional development
— program evaluation   — expert testimony
— organizational development   — public information

This list is somewhat arbitrary and is intended only to illustrate the many ways in which professional service can be performed. The University of Illinois at Urbana-Champaign policy statement (in APPENDIX 4) carries a more detailed and somewhat different typology, for example.

Any such typology likely will indicate the inevitable overlap of professional service with applied research and also with organized instruction. And that inevitable overlap is but evidence of how the traditional division of institutional mission and individual faculty activity into the triad of "teaching, research, and service" is really obsolete and of limited utility. More useful is to look at academic activity as a continuum along which basic and applied research overlap and merge into application and related forms of outreach, which in turn almost inevitably include a formative component that melds into organized instruction. Furthermore, as was mentioned earlier, teaching, research, and professional service are strongly interdependent.

For all these reasons, it is high time that faculty members, like all other professionals, be held accountable and be rewarded for the aggregate of their performance, using an integrated view of their scholarly activity.

THE POLITICS OF NOMENCLATURE

In spite of these limitations of the traditional research/teaching/service triad, its firm entrenchment in the nomenclature of the academy makes it advisable still to use the term "service," if modified by "professional," in this monograph. However, in redefining what is meant by "service," the hope here is that the insistence on **professional expertise** sufficiently distinguishes professional service from other activities performed by faculty that, though valuable, do not constitute a scholarly pursuit. Such other activities include **institutional citizenship** such as committee work, student advising, and other forms of participation in institutional operation; and **disciplinary citizenship** such as contributions to the operation of a disciplinary or professional association. And that the stress on institutional mission further distinguishes professional service from **civic contributions** such as election to office, jury duty, or voluntarism with religious, philanthropic, and other nonprofit organizations. An internal report of the Public Service Roundtable at the University of North Carolina at Chapel Hill (excerpted in APPENDIX 2) calls this third kind of activity "private service."

Of course, the contributions a faculty member makes to governance, student support, and so on labeled above as "institutional citizenship" are essential to the proper functioning of any college or university. They can demand substantial faculty time and energy, and should be recognized as doing so in considerations of faculty workload. Academic institutions rightly can expect reasonable participation from their faculties, and they should recognize contributions of unusual scope and quality by appropriate honors and awards.

But such involvement of faculty in the operation of the institution should be considered as distinct from the outreach — and teaching, and research — they perform on the basis of their professional expertise. Such professional expertise most commonly is based on a thorough and up-to-date knowledge of a discipline, a professional field, or at times a multidisciplinary problem area; but, that expertise can also derive from being a specialist in an appropriate methodology, such as, for example, distance learning or educational software development. These methodological kinds of expertise lend themselves particularly to what Louise Phelps has called "internal outreach" activities, *where faculty members serve as expert consultants and advisors to other faculty or administrators, applying professional expertise within the institution in a way that parallels external professional service* (1995).

Some in higher education who are deeply committed to greater institutional and individual emphasis on the kind of activity that is the subject of this monograph warn against any use of the term "service" to describe it. They view the term as irreparably tainted by its identification with institutional and disciplinary citizenship and with "doing good" by means of civic contributions. Because of that, they claim, anything called "professional service," in spite of the qualifying adjective, will never be taken seriously in academic circles.

Michigan State, for example, is explicitly rejecting the traditional categories of faculty work and, instead, is making a primary distinction between activities carried out on campus and those targeted primarily at external audiences. Within that context, the MSU report (excerpted in APPENDIX 1) speaks of "outreach," which it defines as

a form of scholarship that cuts across teaching, research, and service. It involves generating, transmitting, applying, and preserving knowledge for the direct benefit of external audiences in ways that are consistent with university and unit missions.

In a similar vein, the UNC at Chapel Hill's School of Public Health lists teaching, research, and "practice" as the components of faculty activity to be considered in its system of promotion and tenure (see APPENDIX 3). This is a very good way of articulating the grounding in professional expertise that distinguishes what this monograph calls "professional service."

The University of Illinois at Urbana-Champaign and some other institutions use the term "public service"; but "professional service" seems to avoid a further potential for confusion. That is, many people, inside and outside higher education, equate "public" with activities involving only public-sector agencies; some even limit the term "public" to *pro bono* work. However, both the societal and the institutional benefits described in earlier sections of this monograph accrue from services provided to the public as well as private sectors, and to paying as well as nonpaying clients. Any of these can meet the criterion of contribution to "the public welfare or the common good" — as long as the work is in the public domain and not classified or proprietary. Furthermore,

> Some in higher education warn against any use of the term "service" to describe it. They view the term as irreparably tainted.

although the nature of the recipients and their ability to pay can affect what choices an institution makes about priorities in the service area, those factors do not affect the intrinsic scholarly or intellectual quality of the work.

Much confusion exists, as well, with regard to whether **individual compensation** to the faculty member for his or her professional service alters the nature of the work or its treatment in a faculty reward system. Some argue that to consider compensated professional service in a faculty reward system constitutes "double-dipping," by adding internal rewards to external compensation.

But that argument is just wrong, and has been rejected by many thoughtful campuses, among them UNC at Chapel Hill (see APPENDIX 2). The issue of individual faculty compensation for professional service, though important in itself, is not germane to a definition of professional service, to its evaluation, or to faculty advancement. Whether a faculty member has been compensated for professional outreach (with money or released time) should not be relevant to "counting" such service in reviews for appointment, promotion, and tenure. Such review decisions recognize an individual faculty member's intellectual qualities and accomplishments, and his or her promise for continuing scholarly activities; the issue of payment is irrelevant to that recognition.

After all, whether or not a faculty member receives extra summer compensation for research activities, or for teaching a summer or evening course, has no bearing on the quality of that research or teaching. The scholarship manifested by authoring a book is not decreased by the royalties it earns — indeed, high sales may well be taken as an indicator of quality. By the same token, then, the intellectual value of professional service does not depend on whether or not the faculty member received an honorarium as a consultant. ☐

Professional Service as A Scholarly Activity

Professional service should and can be an important element in the definition of faculty roles and rewards — but not only because of its societal and institutional benefits. It also can constitute scholarship of the highest order, equivalent in intellectual challenge, creativity, and importance to scholarly research and scholarly teaching. As Elman and I stated in *New Priorities for the University,*

> one can more successfully encourage a wider range of professional activities if these are recognized as valid components of scholarship . . . *[externally oriented] professional activity is an* extension *of traditional scholarship, not a* substitute *for it* (Lynton and Elman, 1987, p. 147-8).

Professional service at its best requires, in the terms of Boyer and Rice, the scholarship of integration, the scholarship of application, the scholarship of teaching, and, yes, also the scholarship of discovery (Boyer, 1990; Rice, 1991).

Professional service has in recent decades been slighted, in part, as was described earlier, because it generally has been lumped together — and confused — with activities of institutional, disciplinary, and other citizenship. However important and worthwhile such activities might be, they are not in first instance based on an individual's scholarly expertise.

Other critics slight the value of professional service even if it is solidly grounded in scholarly expertise because they make an artificial distinction between the *discovery* of knowledge and its *application* — a distinction that is, in fact, false.

In the first place, the synthesis of knowledge that is essential to effective application of that knowledge poses intellectual challenges comparable with those of its creation. In the second, and even more important, when professional service is truly scholarly, a two-way flow of knowledge exists, to and from the locus of application. And the sections that follow will indicate repeatedly how contributions to a discipline can take place in the context of application.

In its five case study descriptions (see **MAKING THE CASE**), this monograph contains examples of outreach projects that demonstrate how professional service can have the attributes of scholarship. These attributes, in turn, suggest a set of measures by which the existence as well as the quality of the scholarship in professional service can be assessed.

To date. colleges and universities often have failed to recognize the potential for scholarship in professional service because they have not paid attention to the **intellectual process** that can characterize this kind of faculty work just as it does scholarly research and scholarly teaching. Shulman (1993, p. 6) reminds us that "'Discipline' is . . . a powerful pun because it not only denotes a domain but also suggests a process: a community that disciplines is one that exercises quality, control, judgment, evaluation, and paradigmatic definition." Similarly, Slevin (1994) has argued that during the past century, the meaning of the term *discipline* has been diminished into a "spatial object, with perimeters that contain a specialized knowledge, method, and dialogue. Disciplines are thus defined by their boundaries." He urges a return to an earlier conception of *discipline* as a **process**: "the act of inviting and enabling others into [a professional conversation about knowledge]." That conception was always the essence of teaching; it is also central to professional service. Both scholarly activities, paraphrasing Slevin, are intellectual work located in the encounter with student or client and in the projects that arise from that encounter.

The Distinct Project as Unit of Assessment

To recognize and evaluate this intellectual work in professional service requires a focus on projects of sufficient substance and duration so as to provide an adequate unit of assessment. As is the case in other dimensions of faculty scholarship, the quality of professional service can best be demonstrated by looking at distinct projects, with goals that can be defined, a context as well as methods that can be described, and outcomes that can be identified. Distinct projects provide the primary measure of a scholar's work within the context of that scholar's activities over time.

Choosing a distinct project as a unit of assessment also provides a way of distinguishing between ongoing conscientious but repetitive activities, on the one hand, and instances of significantly creative work, on the other. All aspects of faculty work, be they research, teaching, or professional service, of necessity include much of the former — but it is the latter that has the potential fully to meet the standards of scholarship.

To focus on distinct projects is particularly important when it is professional service being assessed. Professional service occurs in a variety of formats, including one-shot, in-and-out consultations; single lectures, workshops, or seminars; ongoing consultation as an advisor; and extensive projects. But to lump all of these together can trivialize the entire category of professional service and hide its potential intellectual challenge and scholarly nature. For faculty evaluation, a much clearer distinction needs to be made between the minor professional outreach activities in which a faculty member might be engaged, and the specific, substantive projects that can serve as principal units of assessment.

For example, as part of collaboration between a university and a school system, a faculty member often makes him or herself available to school-based colleagues for consultation and discussion; such ongoing interaction is important and should be recognized as part of that individual's workload if the interaction takes a substantial amount of time. The same is true for a lot of other useful but repetitive professional service activity, such as multiple presentations of a workshop or brief trouble-shooting applications of standard remedies in response to a client's distress call. But such work is not, by itself, the stuff of scholarship. □

MAKING THE CASE

This section contains abbreviated case studies for five illustrative professional service projects. The projects span a range of fields, from ethics to engineering, and a variety of clients, from a professional society to a manufacturing company. Some of the projects were the work of an individual faculty member; others involved more than one person. Some were fee-for-service, paid to the individual faculty member; others carried released time, made possible by a grant or contract; one was partly *pro bono*.

Notwithstanding this variety, the five illustrate only a few of the kinds of professional service suggested on page 17. Many other kinds could have been chosen, had space permitted. The hope is that readers will be able to extrapolate from this limited set to the many other ways in which professional service can be carried out. Further, the five selected are intended not as stellar performances but rather as examples of good practice, worthy of recognition as solid scholarly contributions.

THE ATTRIBUTES OF SCHOLARSHIP

The first goal in presenting these abbreviated case studies is to provide examples of professional service projects as scholarly activities. What, then, do they tell us about the ways in which professional service can be a manifestation of scholarship? What common elements of the scholarly process do they illustrate?

The first is the essential — indeed, perhaps the *defining* — characteristic of all scholarship: It is the **antithesis of rote and routine**. Scholarship is a habit of the mind. It is reflected in the individual faculty member's approach to professional activity. Scholarly work is not carrying out a recurring task according to a prescribed protocol, applying standard methodologies. What unifies the activities of a scholar, whether engaged in teaching, research, or professional service, is an approach to each task as a novel situation, a voyage of exploration into the partially unknown.

The scholar takes a fresh look at every task, identifies what is situation-specific in each project and therefore chooses an approach that is in some measure different from what has been tried before, reflects on the ongoing process, makes corrections as necessary, assesses the outcome, and draws appropriate inferences to inform future work. As a result, each instance of scholarly professional service is likely to have, as well, an element of **discovery and originality**. The scholar **learns from the activity** and has the obligation to **share** this in some appropriate form with colleagues.

The learning that occurs can contribute to knowledge in two ways. It can advance the theoretical or conceptual knowledge base of the discipline — as is illustrated in the public history, ethics, and engineering cases. And, it can contribute to the practice or methodology of professional service — as is illustrated in all five examples — in that each project's methods and procedures themselves constitute innovations or extensions of existing practice.

In the examples, these attributes of scholarship in professional service can be seen in greater detail.

In the examples, these attributes of scholarship in professional service can be seen in greater detail.

The first case, describing the development of a history of the accounting profession in Arizona, is an excellent illustration of how scholars **identify and respond to the singular aspects of a situation.** The history's authors could have taken a very routine approach to the task, producing a straightforward, chronological account of the profession's founding and subsequent growth; indeed, that is what the sponsors wanted. But to do so would have constituted little more than the systematic gathering and display of information of interest to a limited audience.

Instead, the authors approached their task *de novo,* placing it within a broader context and looking for its unique aspects. They decided to describe the development of the professional organization "as part of the national history of the accountancy profession and the development of professions generally." They made **a reasoned choice of goals**, consistent with but going beyond the original wishes of the clients, who were involved in and agreed to the change. This same scholarly impulse is evident in the education project, in the assessment of the English language program. There, in consultation with their sponsors, the team responded to the particular conditions of the project by choosing a qualitative approach. In a third case, the geologist set specific goals and objectives to be achieved by his field guides.

Every one of the cases illustrates a second attribute of scholarship: Having decided on a goal, **the scholar chooses methods that fit that objective and are consistent with available resources.** The public historians chose a combination chronological/ thematic approach, and they developed a strategy that combined interviews and archival research to collect the necessary data. The philosopher decided on a case-based approach; the geologist on an inquiry-based guide; the engineer on a combination of lab tests and plant experiments; the program assessors chose a mix of focus groups and in-depth interviews. In all cases, the project strategy was designed to achieve optimal results within the limitations of time, money, and resources.

All of the cases also are examples of how **the scholar reflects** on her or his work, observing, assessing, and making adjustments as it progresses. In the engineering case, for example, initial lab tests and plant experiments yielded unexpected results that triggered new and innovative approaches. The philosopher found it necessary to modify his instructor-centered style; further, he came to realize that his goal should be not to teach "a course in ethical theory" but rather to help police officers to apply ethical concepts to the situations they confronted in their work in "a structured reasoning process that hinged on the use of moral concepts of evaluation." The public historians discovered a major gap in available materials, and changed their strategy of data gathering. In the program assessment, the questions for in-depth interviews evolved continuously from the focus group sessions. And the geologist responded to feedback by introducing a structured summary to each field trip. Each time, the scholars recognized when and attempted to understand why adjustments were necessary: the unexpected happened or the expected did not.

At the end of a project, a scholar **reflects on outcomes**, trying to evaluate the results, draw inferences, and gain new insights that are generalizable, with the aim of furthering the discipline or the methodology of its application. Thus, every professional service project that is carried out in a scholarly fashion is a **process of inquiry and learning** for the scholar — not just, one hopes, a contribution to the understanding and capabilities of the client. The public historians found a general way of placing a specific history into a broader historical context. The philosopher was able to recognize a number of generalizable ethical standards; the engineer fashioned a technical innovation applicable to other manufacturing situations. The program assessors were able to identify a number of factors affecting the program's impact on its participants and to make recommendations regarding the design of future activities. All the projects also resulted in innovations or improvements in service methodology or practice.

Finally, in each of the examples, the scholar **shared with colleagues** what was learned. In some cases, this sharing took the form of formal publications; in others, it was more informal and local. Sharing is important both because it provides an opportunity for validation of the scholarly nature of the work by colleagues and because dissemination is central to the nature of scholarship. While proprietary or classified work can have high intellectual value, it becomes scholarly professional service only once it can be freely shared.

DOCUMENTATION

The second purpose of the five case studies is to indicate how faculty members might document their cases for the scholarly nature of their professional service projects.

"Making the case" was chosen specifically to connote that the individual must be an active participant, not a passive object, in the documentation of the intellectual process. Merely accumulating papers, reports, and other "products" of the activity is not sufficient. The faculty member must take the lead in articulating a case that makes sense of the scholarship of professional service. This must be done by taking the reader of that documentation along on the journey from intention through enactment to results.

Materials for the case to be made must be gathered throughout the progress of the project. Scholars engaged in professional service should keep an ongoing record of activities, just as they would in a research project, gathering pertinent artifacts and maintaining a log of their reflections. And they need to build in explicit ways of monitoring progress and assessing results. The University of Illinois at Urbana-Champaign policy statement advises faculty members that

> [i]f public service activities are to be used to support a favorable promotion decision, they should be planned with that use in mind . . . and [designed] for qualitative evaluation. . . . [E]valuation should be included as part of the planning of any [public service] activity (see APPENDIX 4).

Adequate documentation of a professional service project must include both *what* was done and *how*; it must also explain *why* specific goals, methods, and resources were chosen for the particular activity being described.

These multiple objectives can be met only by an interrelated combination of pertinent work samples and products, together with a narrative explication of them — an assemblage usually described as a "dossier" or "portfolio." As Edgerton et al. said of the teaching portfolio,

> samples of actual work don't speak for themselves. . . . What's missing — what's needed — is an explanation. . . . General reflection, divorced from evidence of actual performance, fails to capture the situated nature of teaching. . . . But work samples plus reflection make a powerful formula (1991, p. 9).

This personal narrative or statement is important because, as Edgerton et al. point out, again regarding the teaching portfolio,

> good teaching was highly situational. Teachers were not simply good "in general."

Whether they were good or not depended on the particulars *of the situation — exactly what was being taught to whom and under what conditions* (p. 9).

Professional service is equally as situational as teaching. Its quality cannot be assessed without an understanding of the context of the activity, the conditions and constraints under which it was carried out, and the resources that were available.

The Personal Statement. The five case studies reproduced, though abbreviated and incomplete, are examples of such narratives, each with its own voice and its own emphases. But all, in one fashion or another, address most of the following:

▶ The *context* of the activity — the nature and the needs of the client, available resources, and the environment in which the activity took place.

▶ The scholarly *expertise* brought to the project.

▶ The *goals* of the activity.

▶ The scholar's *choice of method and resources* used in carrying out the activity, following its progress, and assessing its outcomes.

▶ The results of the scholar's ongoing *reflection,* describing unique and unexpected features encountered, adaptations made, inferences drawn, and lessons learned.

▶ The *impact* of the work on the scholar's subsequent professional service, teaching, and research activities.

▶ A *self-evaluation* of the perceived outcomes and their implications.

In this last item, it is particularly important that the self-evaluation be a critical analysis of the project and include, where appropriate, descriptions of any false starts and mistakes and what was learned from them. Such missteps often provide excellent evidence of the faculty member's understanding and creativity.

Work Samples and Products. The work samples and products are evidence of what actually took place. How useful these materials are depends on the extent to which they are discussed and reflected upon in the personal statement. For example, the explanation by the public historian as to the kind of information he considered germane

> **Professional service is equally as situational as teaching. Its quality cannot be assessed without an understanding of the context of the activity.**

to the project could be illustrated by sample interview protocols, lists of individuals interviewed, and annotated examples of archival sources consulted. Transcripts of interviews and focus groups are pertinent also for the program assessment case. Similarly, the philosopher's description of the developmental goals and methods of his ethics project could be supplemented by examples of actual syllabi, cases, and participant work; and the work of the engineer, by a description of key tests and experiments and of the seminar for employees.

Products would, in most cases, consist of final reports accompanied by available evidence of impact, such as data about the client's enhanced capabilities or improved performance; enumeration of any follow-up grants awarded; or invitations to provide similar services to others. Any publications resulting from a project of course constitute important products, as would evidence of course revisions resulting from a professional service project and reports generated by assisting students.

Each of the five cases lists a number of possible work samples and products pertinent to the project, although this monograph does not include any actual examples.

EXTERNAL EVALUATIONS

External evaluations make up the third major component of the portfolio or dossier to be assembled: evaluation of the quality and significance of both process and product of the work, provided by those intended to benefit from it and by others qualified to judge it.

While self-evaluation, which should be part of any personal statement, is obviously the responsibility of the faculty member, the principal responsibility for gathering the necessary evaluatory material shifts to the department chair, unit head, or dean responsible for the initial steps in the faculty review process. Broadly speaking, three sources exist for external evaluation:

▶ The *primary audience* — that is, the direct target(s) of the activity, whose skills and understanding were to be enhanced or whose working conditions were to be improved by the project. In traditional instruction, students are the primary audience; in professional service, the primary audience would be, for example, the technical staff and other personnel on the factory floor affected by the engineering project, the trainers and police officers in the ethics project, the members of the professional accountancy association in the public history project, and the participants in the English language program in the education project. In each case, this direct audience could comment on matters such as the faculty member's preparation, presentation, and pertinence, as well as the impact the project had on them.

▶ The *client(s) or sponsor(s)* of the activity — who can evaluate the extent to which the faculty member's work met the intended goals and the client's needs. Examples here are the officers of the accountancy association; the managers of the engineering company; the sponsors of the police ethics program, the academy administrators, and perhaps the supervising police chiefs; and the sponsors of the language program. Often, this category overlaps with the first: In the engineering project, for example, company managers were both the clients and, to some measure, the primary audience.

Academic administrators and faculty colleagues from within the college or university also fall into this second category. They can, for example, comment on the extent to which the work furthered institutional and unit missions and benefitted other activities, and also how its innovations or methodology might improve their own professional service practice.

▶ *Experts* in the subject matter and/or the methodology of the activity — who can evaluate the faculty member's work in terms of the norms of the pertinent field and can speak to the originality of the process and the significance of the outcomes. In this category, care must be taken to elicit opinions from content specialists, who can assess any contributions of the project to the discipline, *and* from persons knowledgeable about process and application, who can speak to the extent to which the project has improved methodology. For the ethics project, for example, evaluations should be sought both from philosophers specializing in the subject and from persons with experience in the kind of outreach represented by the work.

When those charged with the review of the individual faculty member's scholarship solicit such external evaluations, it is important that the solicitation explicitly describe what information is sought, and the measures by which the work will be assessed.

EXAMPLES OF BEST WORK

The extensive documentation described here clearly demands a great deal of time, both from the individual faculty member preparing the material and from those called upon to review it. That circumstance alone constitutes a good practical reason why full documentation should be provided only for examples of best work, as selected by the individual under review.

An even more significant reason to compile only a selective dossier is that to do so shifts the emphasis from **quantity** to **quality**. Former president Donald Kennedy of Stanford University has been eloquent in making the case for a selective approach to assessment. In his March 1991 *Essay to the Stanford Community,* he came out very strongly against "the quantitative use of research output as a criterion for appointment and promotion," calling this "a bankrupt idea." He recommended that

> *to reverse the appalling belief that counting and weighing are important parts of evaluation . . . Stanford should limit the number of publications that can be considered in appointment and promotion* (p. 4).

The same argument can be made for professional service (and also for teaching).

* * *

The five cases — public history, geology, ethics, engineering, and education — follow . . .

Case Study: Public History

A PROJECT IN THE PRACTICE OF PUBLIC HISTORY

Described by Noel Stowe, professor of history and acting dean of the graduate school, Arizona State University

What We Did and Why

This project began as a request from the state CPA society to write the history of the society to celebrate its emergence as a major professional organization. The society proposed to pay a fee and expenses for the research and writing, open its records, ask key members for interviews, and press the state accountancy board to likewise open its records.

Our early discussion focused on the design of the project and the final manuscript for the book. The society wanted a conventional history, beginning with the origins of the profession in Arizona, and chapter by chapter describing the history and role of the professional society in getting to where it was today. We wanted to expand the scope of the project to trace the appearance and early development of the accountancy profession in the state as a part of its development locally into regional and national contexts.

Initially, we proposed a topical outline, examining themes that explained how the society and the profession had grown and become so successful over time. When the society rejected that and insisted instead on a chronological approach, we recast its ideas along a different dimension and proposed discussing the society and state profession as part of the national history of the accountancy profession and the development of professions generally. Such an approach permitted beginning in the nineteenth century with this topic, explaining the beginnings of the profession in the state in its most rudimentary form, and explaining the natural unfolding of the profession into its more complex manifestations. This lifted the project out of the inherent parochialism of a chronological design, and assisted in dealing with the legislative and regulatory history of the profession, which otherwise would appear extraordinarily pedantic, pedestrian, and at times petty-politics personified.

Recasting the project in a new form drew upon our backgrounds, which enabled us to give the history a dimension that asked questions about the state CPA society from a contemporary viewpoint. We sought clues to understand how that society had emerged from its past, and how it came to be what it was in the present. We had to understand the entire historical framework, which came to consist of overlays of state, professional, and society events and people, and which had to fit within a twentieth century marked by rapid change. We hit upon a strategy of discussing the history of the profession and the history of the society within the thematic framework of the Americanization of Arizona in the late-nineteenth and early-twentieth centuries, the meaning of statehood following 1912, and the unfolding and evolving professionalization of accountancy itself. Our accountancy-history discussion had to accommodate and fit among a series of converging histories.

At the outset of the project, we were startled to discover that the staff at the office of the State Accountancy Board, which had been presumed to be holding the bulk of our documentation, had routinely been destroying office records under a state records-retention program. All material and all correspondence covering the early development of the profession were gone. The project's credibility now relied on a different, less numerous, and less rich documentation. The major challenge was to rethink how to handle the research work, especially handling the early years. Our chronological discussion examining the facets of professionalization had to be combined with a topical approach, with each chapter reconceived around a particular theme. This would permit us to draw assumptions about decisions and trends and hypothesize about how particular decisions and events had evolved.

Making the Case: Outcomes

The innovative aspects of the project lay in conceptualizing, drawing assumptions, and hypothesizing about historical decisions and events. Combining the theme of professionalization with a discussion of the legislative history of the profession, the appearance of the State Board, the emergence of a tight-knit professional society, and the final evolution of a large impersonal professional organization required our drawing on a number of skills and practices learned in previous research work. The innovation lay in reconstructing a local history and lifting it out of an anecdotal, antiquarian context and making sense of local history in wider contexts.

The project provided a history of the society for its members; it enables them to better appreciate the emergence of their state profession with a national context; it places a state's professionalization trend within a national twentieth-century perspective, and an otherwise parochial local setting back into that framework. For a state having a largely transplanted population, a reading of this book permits members of a professional group to understand their history within a national backdrop.

The particular project incorporated in a limited way the work of one research assistant, who delved into a survey of some published local records. The conceptualization problems encountered and the paucity of research materials indirectly have helped in our designing of a graduate research methods class and selecting of reading material on historical methodology.

Until the appearance of our history, there was virtually no published information on professionalization among the state's professions, e.g., law, medicine, engineering. With our project, we offer a model of how to approach a history of the other professions within the state in a way that avoids the approach of being just a chronology of an organization.

Making the Case: Work Samples and Products

The scope of our work can be illustrated by work samples such as a summary of the many interviews conducted, an outline of the principal questions raised in these encounters, and a listing of the principal archival and other sources consulted. We would add, as well, sample syllabi and reading lists from graduate courses that have been influenced by this work, with an indication of how they differed from earlier versions.

The state society of CPAs published the manuscript as a book and distributed it widely. The book fills a gap within the bibliography of state history. It also offers a model for other professions within the state and elsewhere of how to approach a history, as well as how to synthesize anecdotes and isolated events into a coherent framework, avoiding a chronicle-like approach. The published book itself is, of course, the principal tangible product.

Making the Case: Evaluations

The two principal sources of evaluation of our work are our clients and our professional colleagues. The former can articulate the extent to which our work met their needs, and also describe how we worked with representatives of the professional society and the extent to which we listened and responded to their comments and suggestions. Individual accountants, both in Arizona and elsewhere, can state whether they found the work interesting, and members of other professions could indicate whether a similar effort would benefit them. Professional colleagues can assess the quality of our work according to the standards of history, and can describe the ways in which the project contributed to the discipline in content and in methodology.

Making the Case: How We Shared What We Learned

Our published report was widely distributed, although we have no way of knowing how widely it was read. We have described our work to fellow public historians at a number of local, regional, and national conferences; and we have spoken about it on campus to the history department, as well as to faculty of the accountancy program. ∎

Case Study: Geology

GEOLOGICAL FIELD STUDY GUIDES

Described by Michael Cummings, professor of geology, Portland State University

What We Did and Why

Improving science and technology literacy in the U.S. is an important goal, as citizens are confronted with an array of scientific discoveries and technological advances. My interests lie in earth science education as a readily accessible route to this literacy. In deciding how to approach this problem, I began early in my career to experiment with different pedagogical techniques in both discipline-related and general-education courses at the university level. My entry into K-12 education in earth science came as an outgrowth of these interests. My early K-12 attempts were rather poorly devised and incoherent; the efforts lasted for short periods and were quickly pushed aside by teaching and research activities.

In 1992, the Cordilleran Section of the Geological Society of America (GSA) asked me to develop a field trip for K-12 teachers, as a first effort of the Section at K-12 educational outreach. I began by setting goals and objectives for the field study. I wanted the participants to investigate sites by gathering data, performing relatively simple calculations, interpreting geologic and topographic data, and discussing the implications of their findings. I did not wish to "lead" this field study; I wanted to be a participant in the process. I also wanted a multidisciplinary approach to problem solutions that would clearly illustrate the connections between science and society.

These objectives required me to rethink traditional field guides, and resulted in my devising an inquiry-based approach that established a framework by which participants could investigate and interpret the site. Four sites visited during two days utilized multidisciplinary skills and became progressively more abstract in their scope.

Preparing this type of guide required me to construct a series of questions that used the specific characteristics of the site to draw out the particular theme I wanted to emphasize. Had I chosen a different objective, I could have constructed a totally different set of questions.

The inquiry-based nature of the field guides was well received and helped participants to work with considerable independence and to defocus their attention from the "leader." Participants became very involved with the investigation of the sites and used the guides as a format to organize their observations. However, evaluations of the initial field studies indicated that the participants wanted a more structured closure to their work at each site, so that they could further integrate their understanding with that of the leader and other participants. I made appropriate changes.

Making the Case: Outcomes

The principal outcome of this project has been to improve the science literacy of K-12 teachers by strengthening their background and confidence, enabling them, in turn, to work more effectively with their classes. My work with high school students as summer apprentices and classroom visits have been two further outgrowths of this original trip.

As a result of this work, an increasing number of individuals are using the format of an inquiry-based field study guide to enhance not only K-12 instruction but also undergraduate and graduate teaching. The format was used during a National Science Foundation-sponsored two-week Undergraduate Faculty Enhancement Workshop, attended by twenty-three undergraduate faculty, two K-12 teachers (high school and middle school), three high school students, and two undergraduates. The inquiry-based format was subsequently used by some of these participants for their own field studies, and has served as a model for developing field guides at several meetings of the Cordilleran Section. I am preparing for publication a paper describing their design and use that I presented at a national meeting of the GSA.

My development of the inquiry-based field guides has led to substantial modification of my teaching approaches both in the field and in the classroom. I now use this format for most field studies and have modified my classes for nonscience majors as well as geology majors to include more hands-on investigative activities.

The project and its direct outcomes have had further impact on my personal activities. I was asked to chair the Education Committee of the Cordilleran Section of the GSA America. This position also placed me on the Education Committee of the GSA; representing that committee, I served on a two-person working group that wrote the original document to examine faculty roles and rewards as part of the Syracuse University Project [see Diamond and Adam, eds.]. Also, I now am serving on a committee that will review the National Research Council standards for K-12 science education.

At the local level, I have increased my interest in involving K-12 teachers and high school, undergraduate, and graduate students in my research activities. I also have been successful in obtaining Undergraduate Faculty Enhancement and Research Experiences for Undergraduates grants through the National Science Foundation. I have small grants and contracts through the Port of Portland and the Bureau of Land Management that involve undergraduates, K-12 teachers, and high school students in environmental research problems. I am a coprincipal investigator on a grant for improving science education offerings for preservice middle school teachers in the Portland metropolitan area. We have received a seed grant from the National Science Foundation and are now preparing the final proposal.

Because of the deteriorating funding picture at all levels of education, I have been particularly concerned in this work to develop low-cost activities that are accessible to teachers and yet produce fundamental changes in attitudes and approaches. I now work carefully to link and utilize whatever resources are available to further my efforts. This includes inviting K-12 teachers and their students to participate with us in research projects, field studies, and programs offered through the Department of Geology. This allows me to keep costs low and to effectively utilize available resources. It also allows me to integrate educators and students and to improve the seamless delivery of educational services.

Making the Case: Work Samples and Products

Work samples that document this project could include copies of the field guides and of other materials distributed or available to the participants, such as geological and topographic maps and other site descriptions. Participant responses to the questions posed about each site also would be included. Subsequent versions of field guides as well as the paper I presented to the GSA would figure among the products, as would materials developed on the basis of this work for my undergraduate and graduate courses.

Making the Case: Evaluations

Evaluations of these efforts could come in many forms. In all my programs, I ask participants to evaluate the experience and how the program has modified their approach to science and science education. Depending upon the objectives of the program, these evaluations provide me with direct feedback that allows modification of subsequent offerings. Since the experimentation I am doing with pedagogical methods is integrated into grant proposals, these methods are evaluated by granting agencies that approve funding for continued practice and design of educational outreach programs.

Comments by peer-reviewers of any papers I submitted for publication and abstracts accepted at professional meetings could provide other evaluations.

Inquiry-based field study guides now are used by some participants in the Undergraduate Faculty Enhancement workshop, and I am receiving their comments by e-mail.

The most difficult to assess is the long-term impact on teachers, students, and the community. This impact takes many years and is particularly difficult to define.

Making the Case: How I Shared What I Learned

I have shared what I learned by providing opportunities for more educators to experience inquiry-based field guides. This has included workshops, talks, and course offerings. In addition, I have discussed these approaches with junior faculty and postdoctoral research fellows at various universities and colleges, and have encouraged them to examine the methods and provided them with materials that they can adapt for their purposes. I always involve undergraduates and graduate students in these educational programs, and have provided opportunities for preservice teachers to obtain credit by working with me on the general-education courses that I have developed. ■

Case Study: Ethics

ETHICS INSTRUCTION IN POLICE ACADEMIES

Described by Howard Cohen, previously associate professor of philosophy, University of Massachusetts at Boston; currently interim provost, University of Wisconsin-Parkside

What I Did and Why

For a number of years, I have been developing curricula for ethics instruction in police academies. This work grew out of my research and teaching interests in authority relationships. Teaching a six-week seminar during the first summer of a five-year, NEH-funded project to provide ethics seminars gave me the opportunity to explore the situations that the police practitioners reported as raising ethical problems. My approach was to have participants describe their experience, to explain moral concepts and terms of evaluation to them, and to have us work together to apply concepts to cases. In the course of the subsequent summers of the five-year project, we developed a curriculum to be used by trainers at the academies that was based on analysis of cases — taking the trainers through a structured reasoning process that hinged on the use of moral concepts of evaluation.

The most significant change in my seminar design as it developed over time was that I came to understand that it was not productive to teach police a variety of moral theories and to treat their cases as illustrations of theoretical points. That is, in fact, the way many applied ethics courses were taught at the time. Early on, I tried this in the Institute Seminars, but I soon realized that the participants were not there for a course in ethical theory.

I also changed my teaching method in the course of the project. When I started teaching police ethics seminars, I was wedded to a combination lecture/discussion technique. I was more or less always at the center of the conversation in class. This seemed to work well in 50-minute classes, and I was able to engage large numbers of students in the discussion, but the bottom line was that I was performing for the whole time. This method started to break down when I tried to transfer it to three-hour sessions, and it was impossible for longer days.

What I discovered was that I could teach more effectively by organizing small-group discussion around examples for analysis or structured exercises designed to use key theoretical concepts. I ended up writing a number of these for my training sessions.

Making the Case: Outcomes

The principal outcome of these five years of institutes was an approach to curriculum design for ethics instruction in police academies. Participants developed and learned how to teach integrated ethics modules based on case discussion, tailored to the participants' home circumstances, and generally integrated into other components of the academy curriculum. This was an advance over what had existed previously: first, because ethics rarely came up in police training; second, because recruits were encouraged to discuss and explore their options in this curriculum. For the most part, police training was a matter of learning policy and obeying commands; discussion was not encouraged. I was able to convince many trainers that mine was a better way to address the moral concerns of recruits, not to mention of veteran officers.

At the conclusion of this project, I had become familiar enough with the moral issues of policing and the problems inherent in trying to teach ethics to police officers that the theoretical basis of what I was trying to accomplish became clear to me. I was able to develop a set of standards of good policing that were derived from social contract theory, but that had enough specificity to serve as standards of evaluation in particular cases. These standards eventually became the theoretical core of a book, *Power and Restraint*. To my mind, this is an original contribution to knowledge — it draws connections that were not previously understood, and it addresses a neglected problem in political theory: What are the obligations of those who accept the authority to govern?

The work also has had an impact on my regular, campus-based teaching. After a while, I started to use the training session techniques in my classroom teaching. I designed exercises and examples for my classes, using small groups at least once and sometimes more in every class period. I believe that students find this technique much more engaging, and it really improves class discussion. Once a topic has been worked over in small groups, we reassemble to discuss it together. Discussions are more sophisticated, ideas have already been tested, students who are typically reluctant to participate are able to do so, and I still have a chance to hear what is being learned and what needs more attention. I have no doubt that my police training experience has made me a better classroom teacher.

The most important potential outcome is also the most difficult to assess: the impact on the professional behavior of the police officers who have taken ethics instruction according to the model I developed. The participating trainers were tested at the end of the course by being asked to analyze a case. I was pleased with the extent to which most were able to recognize and analyze the key ethical issues. In addition, student feedback, both oral and written during and after the course, was very positive. On the other hand, I have no way to assess whether the ethics instruction resulted in more ethical conduct on the job.

Making the Case: Work Samples and Products

As further documentation of this service contribution, I would pull together a number of "artifacts" of my work: e.g., the syllabus of the curriculum designed, an example of an integrated ethics module, reading lists, and several cases. I also would include a number of cases written and taught by participants, which I used as outcomes assessment, with examples of what I considered good, average, and inadequate performance. In addition, in order to provide a measure of the scope and intensity of the program, I would add a summary of dates and frequency of meeting times and the number of participants, and include copies of the grant application and the yearly and final reports provided to the funding agency.

One could also gather information about the number of police academies and departments that introduced ongoing ethics curricula as a result of our program, including an estimate of the total number of officers participating.

Making the Case: Evaluations

Student evaluations were collected at the end of each summer program. Together with a summary of the results, I would include sample questionnaires (eliciting comments regarding level of preparation, effectiveness of presentation, amount learned, appropriateness to practice, and anticipated impact on the individual's professional work).

In addition, I would suggest to those responsible for assessing my work to solicit evaluations from the following:

▶ Academy heads, police chiefs, trainers, who can comment on the impact of the activity. Did they find the training valuable? Was anything changed as a result of the project?

▶ Other academic professionals engaged in similar activities, who could assess the adequacy of my knowledge base, the appropriateness and originality of my methods, and the impact of the work on the general approach to ethics instruction in law enforcement academies.

▶ Administrators and colleagues in my institution, who could evaluate the impact on teaching, departmental and institutional programs, and mission.

▶ Other philosophers, who can speak to the soundness of my theoretical base, the rigor of my reasoning, and the originality and importance of my conclusions.

Making the Case: How I Shared What I Learned

The contribution to the discipline derived from the project has been summarized in the book mentioned earlier, published after favorable review of the manuscript by a number of experts. I have also given a number of talks on police ethics — some to philosophy departments, some public lectures, and one presentation to a conference of campus police directors. In the presentations to philosophy departments, as well as in many informal ways in discussions with my colleagues, I have shared what I have learned about effective methods of organization, content, and presentation to audiences such as officers in police academies. ■

Case Study: Engineering

IMPROVING A CHEMICAL MANUFACTURING PROCESS

Described by Allan Myerson, professor of chemical engineering and dean of the School of Chemical and Materials Science, New York Polytechnic University

What We Did and Why

A manufacturer of chemicals approached us for help in reducing the impurity content in one of its products. The company, like many others in our region, is too small to support its own in-house applied research and testing capability, and had used our services several times in the past to improve operating procedures in other parts of its activities. This time we were asked to analyze current plant design and operation in order to determine possible modifications in operating procedure so as to minimize the presence of impurities in the product. With the assistance of our Office of Grants and Contracts, we signed an agreement that provided funding for a fraction of my time during a semester and a summer, as well as support for a graduate research assistant and a postdoctoral fellow during that period. It might be of interest to note that my university has a practice plan under which external income of this kind is shared, on a sliding scale, between the institution and the faculty member(s) involved, in return for which the latter can use university computer and lab facilities as well as limited clerical services.

Our approach to the task was to begin by obtaining data and information from the company on current procedures and products, and at the same time to survey and evaluate pertinent literature and patents. On the basis of this preliminary information, we developed a plan to identify the mechanism of pollution and to evaluate a number of promising improvements by means of a combination of lab tests and plant experiments. The latter provided additional plant data, some of which turned out to be quite unexpected. This triggered some reevaluation and replanning of tests and experiments, and led us to some innovative approaches.

Making the Case: Outcomes

The project resulted in a set of explicit recommendations to the company regarding changes in operating procedures as well as plant design. We also developed a computer program to predict operating conditions, which allowed the company to adapt its procedures in an ongoing fashion to possible changes in available raw materials, as well as to changes in product specifications.

At the end of our work, we submitted our findings and recommendations in a detailed written report to the company, and also conducted a day-long seminar for company personnel. The purpose of the seminar was twofold: to introduce the redesigned procedures and the computer program, and also to provide this personnel with a better understanding of pertinent concepts, which would place them in a better position to cope with similar issues in the future. Of course, throughout the project we had worked closely with some of the operating personnel, obtaining a great deal of important information from them while, at the same time, improving their understanding of the process.

The company used our recommendations not only to modify operating procedures in the existing plant but also to design a plant expansion. From our perspective, the project provided excellent hands-on experience both for the postdoctoral fellow and for the graduate student. I have been using the project as a case study in my lectures and courses, and I published a paper in a technical journal on our innovative approach to plant-based experiments.

Making the Case: Work Samples and Products

I've already indicated some of the materials I can pull together in order to illustrate the nature of our project. These include copies or examples of the following:

▶ the company's original statement of need and the agreement subsequently signed;

▶ a description of plant experiments and lab tests;

▶ the final report to the company;

▶ descriptive material regarding the computer program;

▶ an outline of the seminar for plant personnel;

▶ descriptions of modifications and expansions made in the existing plant by the company on the basis of our findings and recommendations;

▶ case studies derived from the project I have used in my instruction;

▶ my published paper;

▶ the project reports prepared by the participating graduate student and the postdoctoral fellow.

Making the Case: Evaluations

Letters of evaluation should be solicited from the following categories of individuals who were involved in one way or another in the project:

▶ the technical personnel in the plant — who can attest to the effectiveness of our interaction during the project, to the impact of the seminar on their understanding, and to the usefulness and reliability of the computer program;

▶ corporate managers — attesting to the impact of the project on their operation, including the decision to expand;

▶ the participating graduate student and postdoc — attesting to the benefits they derived;

▶ students in classes and seminars — who can attest to my utilization of the project as an instructional case study and in other ways;

▶ my colleagues, department chair, dean, and provost — who can judge the impact of the project on the work of the department, college, and institution and its consistency with the institution's mission;

▶ specialists in the appropriate field of chemical engineering — as to the validity and originality of my approach and my conclusions, and as to the project's impact on the field.

Making the Case: How I Shared What I Learned

What I learned from this project falls into two categories. A number of new insights into the particular kind of chemical manufacturing process furthered the discipline, and I shared those with fellow experts by means of a publication in a refereed journal. I also learned a good deal about ways of interacting with clients, at the management and the factory floor levels, and about how to conduct a project of this type.

Also, I have given seminars on the conduct and the methodology of this kind of professional service to members of my College of Engineering and have spoken about it informally with individual colleagues, especially younger members of my department. ■

Case Study: Education

ASSESSMENT OF AN ENGLISH LANGUAGE PROGRAM FOR IMMIGRANTS

Described by Peter Kiang, associate professor of education, University of Massachusetts at Boston

What We Did and Why

The administrators of a statewide English Literacy Demonstration (ELD) Project asked me to carry out a preliminary evaluation of one of their activities: an English Transitional Program (ETP) for recent Chinese immigrants. The program was developed by the Asian American Newcomers Association, together with the Chinese Community Education Council and a nearby community college. The program had been under way for three years, and the sponsors wished to assess how things were going and consider further program development.

The time available for the evaluation was four months. Funding was limited to a fraction of my time and the part-time assistance of three undergraduate students, themselves adults, Chinese-born, and trilingual in Mandarin, Cantonese, and English. These students already were trained in community-based research methods and grounded in their own experiences as ESL adult learners.

Two factors influenced my choice of goals and methods. One was the limitation of time and resources. The other was the great variety in backgrounds, ages, and objectives among the participants in the program. Some entered the program with the clear goal of gaining entry into higher education. Others enrolled to improve their immediate employment opportunities. Another group came to this country already having a college degree but wanting to learn more about American culture and customs. In addition, a number of the participants changed their goals in the course of the program.

Due to this diversity, participants enter, exit, and experience the program in many different ways. It took only a few pilot interviews to show the variation in their views about the program's curricular focus and level of difficulty, the teaching styles of the instructors, and other aspects of the program. Hence, it was not feasible to assess the program on the basis of an explicit set of outcomes.

I discussed these issues with the sponsors, and they agreed that I could use bilingual focus groups and individual interviews to examine qualitatively how participants at various levels perceive and respond to the choices, opportunities, and barriers they experience in the ETP program.

Specific interview questions were developed by the research team, consisting of myself and the three student assistants, based on meetings with the ETP staff; questionnaires designed by the staff of ELD; and, more important, on the evolving process of the research itself. Focus groups conducted at each level of the program guided the development of in-depth interviews. Time and again, the group sessions would raise unexpected issues that we then pursued in the individual interviews. Each interview was taped, transcribed, translated, and analyzed for themes, critical issues, and further questions. Thus, the whole process was one of ongoing reflection and feedback.

The combination of focus groups and interviews brought about intense communication and relationships between our team and the project participants, as well as among the team members. We believe that we were able to gain entry into the day-to-day, complex world of the individual adult learners and, simultaneously, to maintain a systemic, long-term view of the community as a whole.

Making the Case: Outcomes

From the analysis of the interviews and focus groups, we were able to draw a number of inferences regarding external and internal factors affecting the impact of the program. These included dimensions such as the importance of having personal plans at the time of entry into the program, prior work experience and education as an asset, and the contexts of job market and family.

On the basis of our analysis, we were able to identify a number of suggestions for further program development. These included matters such as classroom pedagogy, the role of advising and counseling, the selection process, and the strengthening of community themes in the curriculum.

We also identified areas for further inquiry, that could be pursued under looser time constraints and using a more holistic approach of ethnographic techniques that immerse and ground researchers and practitioners in the concrete worlds and daily lives of the practitioners. This would make possible much richer case studies with more profound implications for continuing program improvement.

A further outcome were the evident intellectual as well as motivational benefits derived by the student assistants on the team. One is now teaching in an elementary school, and the other two are currently applying for graduate study in education and counseling, in part as a result of their participation in the project.

In addition, I obtained a good deal of information that I am incorporating into the syllabi of my courses. I also developed further understanding of evaluation methodologies applicable to situations like the one encountered in this project. I shared the latter with a number of my colleagues engaged in similar professional outreach activities.

Making the Case: Work Samples and Products

Our approach can be illustrated by sample interview protocols and focus group questions, as well as sample transcripts and content analyses. The principal product is a written report to the sponsors, describing the details of the project and containing our conclusions and our recommendations. The final reports the students wrote for me at the end of the project are further products that provide information.

Making the Case: Evaluations

Evaluations of the project should be provided by the sponsors, as to their satisfaction with our work and the extent and quality of our communication with them; from the undergraduate student assistants, as to the adequacy of the guidance they received and the learning that took place; and from ETP participants, as to the quality of the interviews and focus groups, the insightfulness of the questions, and the level of reciprocal communication. In addition, experts in qualitative program evaluation can speak to the adequacy of our methods. Those familiar with similar programs can comment on the significance of our conclusions and recommendations.

Making the Case: How We Shared What We Learned

Key members of the sponsoring agency and of the three organizations delivering the program received copies of our detailed report. A summary of the report was more widely distributed. In addition, we shared copies of the report with a number of academic colleagues, and I presented a seminar on my work to faculty and graduate students on my campus. ∎

ASSESSING THE CASE

Once the elements of a case have been assembled, what then are the **measures** to be applied to assess the quality of a professional service project? What questions should be asked to find out whether a particular activity constituted an outstanding example of scholarship, or just a fairly average one, or perhaps even one that was mediocre?

No quantitative measures exist, nor any one way of articulating qualitative ones. Myriad different choices of words and emphases are possible. What follows is only an example of how a campus might express measures of excellence for an activity whose quality depends as much on process as on outcomes. The scheme offered below differs in detail but is broadly consistent with the measures to be suggested in the forthcoming *Scholarship Assessed* (Boyer, in press).

As a starting point, then, for further discussion on a campus, here is a suggested set of measures to be applied to a professional service project:

▶ depth of the expertise and preparation
▶ appropriateness of chosen goals and methods
▶ effectiveness of communication
▶ quality of reflection
▶ impact
▶ originality and innovation.

It seems self-evident that the quality of scholarship in professional service — as in teaching and in research, as well — depends on the adequacy of the faculty member's **knowledge base and preparation** informing the scholarly process. To apply this measure to a particular project, one would ask: Is the service grounded in the faculty member's professional expertise? Does it draw on up-to-date disciplinary knowledge? Does it indicate adequate preparation through literature searches and other means? Has the faculty member become adequately familiar with the context as well as the constraints influencing the project, and with the nature and the priorities of the client(s)?

An appropriate set of questions for the remaining five measures would be the following:

For the **appropriateness of the choices** made by the scholar as to goals and methods: Are the objectives of the project clear and appropriate to the context and to available resources? Has the faculty member made a good, realistic, and cost-effective choice with regard to the method of carrying out the project?

For the effectiveness of **communication and presentation**: In both the formulation and the implementation of the task, has there been an adequate dialogue between the faculty member and the recipients of the service? Has the faculty member effectively communicated the results of the project to all who should profit from it? Did that communication include acquainting the beneficiaries with the knowledge base they need to profit from the project? Are insights obtained from the project by the faculty member effectively communicated to colleagues?

For each measure, these are the kinds of questions that should be put explicitly to external evaluators.

For the effectiveness and depth of insight manifested in ongoing and concluding **reflection**: Did the project contain adequate ways of monitoring its progress and of assessing its outcomes? Were any unanticipated developments spotted in a timely fashion, and did they lead to constructive adaptations? Did the faculty member draw appropriate inferences from the results?

For the **impact** of the activity: What impact has the project had on its intended beneficiaries? Are those beneficiaries now carrying out their activities more effectively, have they adopted policies and practices more in line with the prevailing knowledge base, and are they better prepared for future activities? Did the project move practice or policy forward in ways that might benefit others, as well? Was this adequately shared in formal and informal ways? Did it further institutional mission? What impact did it have on the faculty member's research and/or on her or his teaching? Did students benefit from direct participation in the service project?

And last, but most certainly not least, for the **originality** and degree of **innovation** manifest in the activity: Was there innovation in the application of disciplinary knowledge and methodology to the particular context of the project? Were any unanticipated developments during the course of the project, and the outcomes of the work, creatively interpreted so as to add to disciplinary knowledge? Did the outcomes and their interpretation constitute an original contribution to the field?

(Of course, even routine applications of knowledge can be useful to the recipients, just as routine teaching can benefit students and routine measurements can yield valid research data. Such activities need to be evaluated on the basis of their usefulness, even though they may not in and of themselves constitute scholarship.)

For each measure, these are the kinds of questions that should be put explicitly to external evaluators, and which the reviewers of the dossier or portfolio should then address on the basis of all the aggregated evidence. A significant benefit of such extended documentation, with its emphasis on process as well as product, is that it enables the faculty member's peers on campus to reach their own conclusions about the quality of faculty work. The assessment by external experts is useful, but it need not be relied on passively.

In this monograph, these measures are not applied to the five projects described earlier in MAKING THE CASE, because as documentation the case studies obviously are abbreviated and incomplete. However, readers are invited to review the five examples with either this set or equivalent measures in mind, and in particular to identify what additional information and documentation would be needed in each instance.

COLLECTIVE WORK

Professional service increasingly is carried out not by a single individual but by a team of specialists from different disciplines, due to the multidisciplinary nature of many of the issues and problems such service addresses. That raises the question of how to assess an individual faculty member's contribution to a collective effort.

On the one hand, in real teamwork it is both impossible and counterproductive to try to parse the enterprise into its components; the whole is greater than the sum of its parts. A solution here would be to view each participant as contributing equally.

On the other, one also can argue that to evaluate a faculty member for academic advancement it is important to assess his or her individual contribution, even to collective efforts, in absolute if not comparative terms. It may not be either possible or useful to know whether one person has brought more or less to the project than the other team members; but it is important to assess whether that person's individual contribution was a sufficiently scholarly one.

Which of these two approaches a college or university should take is a matter of personnel policy to be worked out and decided on each campus. Whatever the outcome, it is evident that the kind of complete, inclusive documentation suggested in this monograph will provide much information regarding the individual faculty member's role in a team effort. The personal statement as well as the evaluations by team members, colleagues, experts, and clients will speak to that issue, especially when the solicitation of those evaluations poses pertinent questions. ☐

AN ACTION AGENDA

A fundamental **change in the culture** of most campuses is needed if professional service is to become, once again, a central part of institutional mission. The principal barrier, at this time, is not just that faculty involvement in such activities is inadequately rewarded in the promotion and tenure process. The problem is more basic, in that professional service (like teaching, in many places) is viewed at best as a laudable deed but not as an intellectually challenging, scholarly activity.

Most campuses lack a climate in which professors talk with colleagues about their professional service activity. As has been repeatedly pointed out in recent years with regard to teaching, only by becoming a topic of public discourse among peers does a faculty activity take its place as a legitimate and valued professional achievement (Shulman, 1993). Professors derive great satisfaction from discussing their scholarly work with their colleagues, and when one speaks of the need to modify the faculty reward system, it is important to realize the value of this kind of recognition.

The inclusive documentation called for in this monograph should be viewed within this context, as well. The rich description of a professional service project provided by personal statement and artifacts is important not just as a basis for evaluation at the time of personnel decisions. It also has great formative value, by providing the basis for collegial discussion to improve the enactment of professional service and, not incidentally, thereby enhancing the esteem in which that activity is held.

Of course, formal recognition of professional service in the promotion and tenure system is critically important, too — not just as an incentive, but most particularly so that faculty involvement in professional service does not become a handicap to career advancement.

Thus, the values reflected at this time in both the informal and the formal faculty reward structure must broaden from their present excessive emphasis on research. That is an essential as well as formidable task. The current automatic equating of scholarship only with research is deeply ingrained in the contemporary academy. Former president of Harvard Derek Bok not long ago complained that

> *research has come to dominate over all other factors in choosing, recognizing, and rewarding faculty* (1991, p. 12).

Tackling this hegemony must be the first item on the action agenda of any college or university wishing to emphasize professional service. It requires, to quote again former president Charles McCallum, of the University of Alabama at Birmingham, *a mix of "top-down" and "bottom-up" strategies. . . . [K]ey officers of a university must make it absolutely clear that community enhancement programs are an* institutional priority — *a must! The leadership of the university . . . must see to it that this refrain of community involvement is sung loudly. . . . [T]he "bottom-up" strategy . . . is essential as a parallel to the administrators' effort. . . . [I]t is faculty who comprise tenure and promotion committees and help set salary guidelines. So this core of the university must reflect an understanding as well as an enthusiastic endorsement of the worth of substantive community activities* (1994, pp. 16, 17).

It is important that each campus generate its own language for describing the characteristics of professional service as a scholarly activity.

For this to happen, faculty and administrators must recognize professional service not only as an external obligation to meet societal needs but also as an internal benefit, as an exciting and creative scholarly activity enriching both teaching and research.

Each college or university engaged in reexamining faculty roles and rewards generally, and the place of professional service specifically, should undertake a thorough exploration and discussion of the nature of scholarship. This should involve appropriate established groups such as promotion and tenure committees, as well as special task forces and public discussion, to ensure that a broad cross section of the faculty and administration participate. The object of the activities should be to have as many interested parties as possible think through what it means to carry out an intellectual task in a scholarly manner. Such thinking applied to professional service can lead to widespread understanding and acceptance of its potential for scholarship.

It is important that each campus generate its own language for describing the characteristics of professional service as a scholarly activity and the set of measures for its evaluation. The version articulated in this monograph is a suggestion, not a prescription; no intention exists here to propose a catechism to be adopted and applied by all institutions. This monograph's is just one of many possible formulations that can be derived from the concept of scholarship as a intellectual process.

For each institution to articulate its own version can happen, again, only through a widely participatory discourse. In larger institutions such as research and comprehensive universities that discourse should take place in each school or college, and in each department or cluster of cognate units within a school or college. The objective of the discussions should be to generate operational terminology specific to each unit and for which the unit feels a degree of ownership. That specificity and ownership is essential if a broader concept of scholarship is to be accepted and the intellectual content of professional service is to be widely recognized and appropriately rewarded. The disciplinary statements regarding the nature of scholarship assembled by Diamond and Adam (to be published by AAHE) should prove very helpful in such a process, as might some questions like those in the box on the next page.

Balancing Institutional Functions and Setting Priorities

The Michigan State University report excerpted in APPENDIX 1 draws attention to some important steps that should be taken by any college or university intending to become engaged more intensively and systematically in professional service.

In the first place, the institution faces

the challenge of balancing these various activities. . . . Maintaining balance involves the thoughtful management of real and enduring tensions.

This balance can be expressed, as in the MSU formulation, as between outreach and nonoutreach activities, or as among professional service, teaching, and research. Whatever terms are used, each institution — and probably also each unit within it — must decide what emphasis should be given to each component so as to be consistent with the nature, history, and context of the institution. Professional service, as this monograph has stressed, should be an important component of almost every college or university because it both meets societal needs and brings internal benefits. But the relative extent of these activities may be quite different in a small, liberal arts college versus a comprehensive university, and in a humanities department versus a social or natural science unit.

Whatever the extent of institutional commitment to professional service, external demand is likely to exceed available resources. Hence, priorities must be set, as they are in other aspects of the institution's activities. Again, from the MSU report:

A close match between faculty expertise and the substantive foci of outreach activity is essential to ensure a robust level of authentically knowledge-based outreach, as well as to integrate outreach into the intellectual fabric of the university.

Ten Questions for Departmental Discussion

Intended to be suggestive and not prescriptive, the questions below might help to structure and facilitate the discourse regarding professional service. They are formulated in terms of a department but, with minor modifications, could be applicable as well to larger units and even to an institution as a whole.

1. What kinds of outreach activities are possible within our discipline or professional field?

2. Which of these activities are particularly consistent with the mission of our school, college, and/or university?

3. Which of these are of greatest potential value in enhancing our department's undergraduate and graduate programs? Which could best provide opportunities for direct student involvement? Which are likely to benefit classroom instruction?

4. Which of these activities are of greatest potential value to, and can most benefit from, basic and applied research carried out by members of the department and related units?

5. In light of our answers to the preceding questions, what should be our collective priorities with regard to professional service provided by members of the department?

6. Do any of these priorities depend on collaboration with other departments? If so, how could that collaboration best be structured?

7. What would we consider to be characteristics of scholarship germane to our discipline or professional field, and how could these characteristics be manifested in professional service?

8. What measures of scholarly quality make sense for us?

9. What documentation would be appropriate for the kind of professional service we want to encourage?

10. How can we best communicate with potential clients of our professional service so as to get their input with regard to needs and priorities?

For each college or university, a number of areas likely exist in which institutional strengths and external needs combine to suggest ways in which "teaching, research, and . . . service can be united in high-profile community-need projects" (McCallum, 1994, p. 16). For some institutions with particular strengths in health-related programs, community health may be such an area. A school or department of management oriented toward small companies and entrepreneurship may find an important outlet in working with moderate-size local businesses. A major emphasis on school-college collaboration may be a particularly promising area elsewhere. Identifying one or more such focal points of activity sets priorities — without, of course, eliminating other potential areas of outreach.

COLLECTIVE RESPONSIBILITY

In essence, this setting of priorities amounts to a translation of the overall campus mission into specific objectives for the units within the institution. Mission statements at the institutional level are, of necessity, broad, and inclusive — and not very helpful in providing guidelines for detailed activity. Such statements, as well as leadership pronouncements about the importance of professional service, become effective only when they are disaggregated into specific terms applicable to individual units within the institution: schools and colleges within comprehensive universities, and in turn departments or other units within schools and colleges. At the departmental or equivalent unit level, general objectives become clearly identified goals and priorities (Diamond and Adam, 1994; Lynton, 1994).

At the departmental or equivalent unit level, general objectives become clearly identified goals and priorities.

Disaggregation of mission to a departmental or equivalent unit level makes it possible to arrive at a specific **profile of collective responsibilities** for the unit. For example, a broad institutional goal to reach out into the community could mean substantial involvement in a school-college collaboration for some departments. For others, it might translate into major contributions to an interdisciplinary structure engaged in applied research and technical assistance, such as an institute for public policy, a program on community health, or a center for small-business development.

For each case, the implications for individual faculty work are quite different, except for one shared consideration: Individual assignments within every unit can vary among faculty members at any given time, and for any one faculty member over time. Each unit should deploy the faculty resources it has available in a differentiated manner so as to achieve an optimal match between its collective needs, on the one hand, and individual faculty strengths and preferences, on the other.

Using collective goals and objectives as the defining framework for faculty activity brings about a subtle but crucial change in the way one looks at the work of a faculty member and the kind of questions asked when reviewing that work for reappointment, promotion, or tenure. Instead of assessing the work of an isolated individual pursuing personal priorities, to be judged without reference to collective needs, one can evaluate the work in terms of that person's contributions to explicit unit objectives. Incentives and rewards for professional service become a matter of departmental, not only individual self-interest, especially if incentives and rewards also are provided to the unit for its collective performance. Wergin (1994), for example, has discussed some of the pertinent issues in moving toward a culture of collective responsibility.

BRIDGING MECHANISMS AND DIALOGUE

Two further steps are needed for outreach to be most effective. One is to establish appropriate bridging mechanisms between the academic institution and its external constituencies. Even a relatively small college, and more certainly a comprehensive university, is quite opaque to anyone on the outside; it is usually difficult to find out what intellectual resources the institution has to offer. Descriptive inventories and directories help, but to make an institution adequately transparent really requires clearly designated and widely publicized contact offices, and staff who can make the connection between an external client and the appropriate faculty member.

That requires not only ready access to information about individual and collective activities on campus, but also an ability to translate between the external formulation of a need and the internal description of an activity. The language a faculty member might use to describe his or her area of expertise is often very different from that a government official, businessperson, or community member would use to express a desire for intervention. A second function of an effective bridging mechanism is to provide the infrastructure and support services necessary to develop contracts or other agreements for professional services.

Closely related to, yet different from this need for transparency is the importance of establishing real dialogue between external clients and internal service providers. External constituents and clients must have a significant and ongoing voice — in setting institutional and unit priorities and in formulating and implementing any professional service activities. Colleges and universities must base their work not just on what they *think* is needed but on what is actually wanted. Often the two will be incongruent. One of the important aspects of professional service as a scholarly activity is the dialogue through which the two are reconciled, as the MSU report points up:

> *To ensure that outreach activities focus on important societal needs . . . all units will want to design thoughtful ways of identifying and setting priorities among problems, frequently through the direct participation of advisory groups representing key external constituencies along with formal needs assessments.*

To enhance its professional service, one final adaptation an institution must undertake is to develop enough organizational flexibility to accommodate multiple, nondisciplinary patterns of response to external needs. That societal problems are not organized by discipline is an old saw, but valid nevertheless. Colleges and universities must establish sufficient structural and budgetary flexibility to encourage cross-cutting activities via centers and institutes, as well as less-formal devices. They also must make sure that faculty involvement in activities located outside the department does not become a handicap when those faculty members are reviewed for advancement. □

A FINAL WORD

The principal purpose of this monograph is to make the case for professional service as an institutional priority and as an important and valued component of faculty scholarly activity. But ultimately, the hope is that American higher education will fully recognize the essential unity and reciprocal relationship among the full range of its knowledge-based tasks. It is time to bury the triad of "teaching, research, and service," with its implication that these are three distinct and different activities that sometimes accidentally reinforce one another — as in, "faculty involvement in research makes for better teaching."

In fact, they are neither distinct nor different, and whatever definitional boundaries might at one time have had some validity are rapidly fading. With more and more field-based and action research, the line between research and professional service is disappearing; and almost every professional service project has an instructional component. In turn, scholarly teaching has a strong element of discovery — indeed, it is itself a form of action research. Differences imputed to the elements of the triad are often more a question of the site of the activity than of its intrinsic nature — instruction in the classroom is called teaching, instruction as part of an outreach project is professional service (Phelps, 1995).

Ultimately, therefore, the purpose of this monograph is to contribute to the mounting chorus of voices stressing the essential similarity of all manifestations of scholarship, and the need to view institutional mission and individual work together, as an integrated, multidimensional whole. It is this whole that represents the knowledge mission of the institution and that reflects the scholarly quality and intellectual vitality of the individual faculty member.

Only by seeing the whole can one arrive at a true measure of multidimensional excellence, and only in that way can institutions as well as individuals gain the flexibility to shape a profile of activities that best matches needs with capabilities. ☐

REFERENCES

Adamany, David. "Science and the Urban University." *Science* 221(1983):427-430.
> *Cf.* also David Adamany. "Sustaining University Values While Reinventing University Commitments to Our Cities." *Universities and Community Schools, A Publication of the University of Pennsylvania* 4(Fall-Winter 1994): 18-22.

Ashby, Eric Lord. "The Case for Ivory Towers." Paper delivered at the International Conference on Higher Education in Tomorrow's World, University of Michigan, Ann Arbor, April 26-29, 1967.

Bok, Derek. *Beyond the Ivory Tower.* Cambridge, MA: Harvard University Press, 1982.

——————. "The Improvement of Teaching." ACLS Occasional Paper. New York: American Council of Learned Societies, 1991.

Boyer, Ernest L. *Scholarship Reconsidered.* Princeton, NJ: Carnegie Foundation for the Advancement of Teaching, 1990.

——————. "Creating the New American College." *The Chronicle of Higher Education,* March 9, 1994, p. A48.

——————. *Scholarship Assessed.* Princeton, NJ: Carnegie Foundation for the Advancement of Teaching, in press.

Bromley, Allan D. "The Other Frontiers of Science." *Science* 215(1982): 1035.

Cavanaugh, Sally Hixon. "Connecting Education and Practice." In *Educating Professionals,* edited by Lynn Curry, Jon Wergin, and Associates. San Francisco: Jossey-Bass, 1993.

Curry, Lynn, Jon Wergin, and Associates, eds. *Educating Professionals.* San Francisco: Jossey-Bass, 1993.

Diamond, Robert M., and Bronwyn E. Adam. "Institutional Mission, Faculty Rewards, and the Emerging Role of the Department Chair." *The Department Chair* 4(Winter 1994): 1, 17-18.

_____ , eds. Manuscript in preparation, American Association for Higher Education, Washington, DC.

Edgerton, Russell, Patricia Hutchings, and Kathleen Quinlan. *The Teaching Portfolio: Capturing the Scholarship in Teaching.* Washington, DC: American Association for Higher Education, 1991.

Ehrlich, Tom. "National and Community Service: The Agenda for Higher Education." Presentation at the Colloquium on National and Community Service, Campus Compact and the American Association for Higher Education, Washington, DC, January 12, 1995.

Elman, Sandra E., and Sue Marx Smock. *Professional Service and Faculty Rewards: Toward an Integrated Structure.* Washington, DC: National Association of State Universities and Land-Grant Colleges, 1985.

Greiner, William R. " 'In the Total of All These Acts': How Can American Universities Address the Urban Agenda?" *Universities and Community Schools, A Publication of the University of Pennsylvania* 4(Fall-Winter 1994): 12-15.

Harkavy, Ira. "University-Community Partnerships: The University of Pennsylvania and West Philadelphia as a Case Study." In *Rethinking Tradition: Integrating Service With Academic Study on College Campuses,* edited by Tamar Y. Kupriec. Denver: Education Commission of the States, 1993.

Harris, Ilene B. "New Expectations for Professional Competence." In *Educating Professionals,* edited by Lynn Curry, Jon Wergin, and Associates. San Francisco: Jossey-Bass, 1993.

Kennedy, Donald. *The Improvement of Teaching, An Essay to the Stanford Community.* Stanford, CA: Stanford University, 1991.

Knefelkamp, L. Lee. "Seasons of Academic Life: Honoring Our Collective Autobiography." *Liberal Education* 76(May/June 1990): 4-11.

Lynton, Ernest A. "A Crisis of Purpose: Reexamining the Role of the University." *Change* 15(Sept/Oct 1983): 18-23, 53.

_____ . "Faculty Roles in the Context of the Departmental Mission." *The Department Chair* 5(Fall 1994): 1, 18-19; corrected version 5(Winter 1995): 8-10.

_____ , and Sandra E. Elman. *New Priorities for the University: Meeting Society's Needs for Applied Knowledge and Competent Individuals.* San Francisco: Jossey-Bass, 1987.

McCallum, Charles A. "The Bottom Line: Broadening the Faculty Reward System." *Universities and Community Schools, A Publication of the University of Pennsylvania* 4(Fall-Winter 1994): 16-17.

Phelps, Louise Wetherbee. "Faculty Service and the Reward System." Presentation at the Third AAHE Conference on Faculty Roles & Rewards, American Association for Higher Education, Phoenix, January 19-22, 1995.

Rice, R. Eugene. "The New American Scholar: Scholarship and the Purposes of the University." *Metropolitan Universities* 1(Spring 1991): 7-18.

_____ , and Laurie Richlin. "Broadening the Conception of Scholarship in the Professions." In *Educating Professionals,* edited by Lynn Curry, Jon Wergin, and Associates. San Francisco: Jossey-Bass, 1993.

Rudolph, Frederic. *The American College and University.* New York: Knopf, 1962.

Schön, Donald A. *The Reflective Practitioner: How Professionals Think in Action.* New York: Basic Books, 1983.

_____ . *Educating the Reflective Practitioner.* San Francisco: Jossey-Bass, 1987.

Shulman, Lee S. "Professing the Liberal Arts." Presentation at the First Institute on Integrating Service With Academic Study, Campus Compact, Stanford, CA, July 1991.

_____ . "Teaching as Community Property." *Change* 25(Nov/Dec 1993): 6–7.

Slevin, James F. "New Definitions of Discipline and the Profession: Implications for the University." Presentation at the National Conference on Higher Education, American Association for Higher Education, Chicago, March 24, 1994.

Votruba, James. Private communication, November 1994.

Wergin, Jon F. *The Collaborative Department: How Five Campuses Are Inching Toward Cultures of Collective Responsibility.* Washington, DC: American Association for Higher Education, 1994.

APPENDIX

1. Michigan State University. *University Outreach at Michigan State University: Extending Knowledge to Serve Society: A Report by The Provost's Committee on University Outreach.* East Lansing, MI: Michigan State University, October 1993.

2. "Summary: Report of the UNC-CH Public Service Roundtable, April 15, 1994." University of North Carolina at Chapel Hill. Photocopy.

3. School of Public Health, University of North Carolina at Chapel Hill. *Appointments, Promotion, and Tenure Manual.* Chapel Hill: School of Public Health, University of North Carolina at Chapel Hill, 1994.

4. Farmer, J.A., and S.F. Schomberg. *A Faculty Guide for Relating Public Service to the Promotion and Tenure Review Process.* Champaign, IL: University of Illinois at Urbana-Champaign, Office of Continuing Education and Public Service, 1993.

APPENDIX

University Outreach at Michigan State University:

Extending Knowledge to Serve Society

A report by
The Provost's Committee on University Outreach

October 1993

THE DEFINING DIMENSIONS OF UNIVERSITY OUTREACH

A Definition of Outreach

Universities exist to generate, transmit, apply, and preserve knowledge. When they do these things for the **direct benefit** of **external** audiences, they are doing university outreach.

The essence of our thinking about outreach is contained in the following definition:

> OUTREACH IS A FORM OF SCHOLARSHIP THAT CUTS ACROSS TEACHING, RESEARCH, AND SERVICE. IT INVOLVES GENERATING, TRANSMITTING, APPLYING, AND PRESERVING KNOWLEDGE FOR THE DIRECT BENEFIT OF EXTERNAL AUDIENCES IN WAYS THAT ARE CONSISTENT WITH UNIVERSITY AND UNIT MISSIONS.

Outreach as a Form of Scholarship

We conceive of outreach as a scholarly activity—it both draws on knowledge developed through other forms of scholarship and contributes to the knowledge base.

Outreach, as are all dimensions of the University's academic mission, is rooted in scholarship. Scholarship is what scholars do; they teach, do research, and serve the University, their disciplines, fields, or professions, and the surrounding society:

- Teaching is a scholarly activity, whether those taught are traditional undergraduate or graduate students taking classes on campus or are traditional or nontraditional students taking classes in off-campus locations during hours set to accommodate their schedules, or in noncredit seminars or workshops reached by modern communication technologies, or in the workplace or community settings through consultation and technical assistance.

- Research is a scholarly activity, whether it is undertaken solely to advance knowledge within a discipline or field, or is intended to respond to pressing problems or issues identified by such external constituencies as local communities, state, national, or international agencies, business or industrial firms, citizen groups, or schools, hospitals, or other public sector and nonprofit organizations.

- Service may be less readily embraced as a scholarly activity, but scholars recognize its importance not only when they serve on university, disciplinary, or professional committees or organizations, but also when they draw on scholarly knowledge to provide medical or therapeutic services, testify before the legislature or Congress, serve on state, national, or international commissions or advisory groups, or work through professional societies to prepare studies and reports on significant societal or global problems.

Teaching, research, and service are simply different expressions of the scholar's central concern: knowledge and its generation, transmission, application, and preservation. When scholars generate knowledge, they discover or create it; when

The Provost's Committee on University Outreach

Universities exist to generate, transmit, apply, and preserve knowledge. When they do these things for the direct benefit of external audiences, they are doing university outreach.

Teaching, research, and service are simply different expressions of the scholar's central concern: knowledge and its generation, transmission, application, and preservation. . . . Outreach covers the full spectrum of knowledge functions.

scholars transmit knowledge they share it with others; when scholars apply knowledge they do so for the purpose of helping others better understand, and sometimes address, circumstances and problems; and when scholars preserve knowledge they seek to save what has been learned for future access.

Outreach can and does cover the full spectrum of knowledge functions. Sometimes outreach involves generating knowledge (e.g., clinical intervention studies). It may also involve transmitting knowledge (e.g., continuing professional education), applying knowledge (e.g., technical assistance), and preserving knowledge (e.g., creating electronically accessible data bases).

In offering this perspective, we fully appreciate that the definition of "scholarship" is a subject of considerable debate in academe. Some scholars argue that scholarship involves discovering or creating new knowledge or, at the very least, synthesizing knowledge in a new way. From this perspective, scholarship is generally synonymous with research. Others offer that communication of one's findings is an important dimension of scholarship. Still others feel that "reflective practice" distinguishes scholarship from non-scholarly, repetitive activities.

The essence of scholarship is the thoughtful creation, interpretation, communication, or use of knowledge that is based in the ideas and methods of recognized disciplines, professions, and interdisciplinary fields.

What, indeed, makes an activity scholarly? At the literal level, as we have asserted, scholarship is what scholars do: they teach, they do research, and they serve their disciplines/professions, the University, and society. But all of us have observed teaching that is not always scholarly, have read research that appears too mechanical to be called scholarship, and have experienced service that has more to do with other attributes than with any scholarly gifts.

We believe that the essence of scholarship is the **thoughtful creation, interpretation, communication, or use of knowledge that is based in the ideas and methods of recognized disciplines, professions, and interdisciplinary fields** What qualifies an activity as "scholarship" is that it be deeply informed by accumulating knowledge in some field, that the knowledge is skillfully interpreted and deployed, and that the activity is carried out with intelligent openness to new information, debate, and criticism.

In our thinking, outreach has the same potential for scholarship as the other major academic functions of the University. This requires the need for a definition that positions outreach at the heart of what the University is and does.

Outreach has the same potential for scholarship as the other major academic functions of the University.

In advancing this conception of outreach, we interpret and apply the thinking embodied in the work of contemporary scholars, such as Ernest Lynton (1992) and Ernest Boyer (1990), who propose an expanded notion of scholarship. For example, although he understands outreach as a separate function and we see it as a cross-cutting function as will be described in the following section, Lynton's (1992:9,14) view of outreach as a scholarly activity parallels our own:

> For pragmatic...as well as substantive reasons, we believe that it is necessary to reexamine prevalent conceptions of what it means to be a scholar. Balance of esteem among research, teaching, and outreach requires the recognition that teaching and outreach not only are essential activities, but that they constitute as much of an intellectual challenge as research, and are equally integral parts of the professional work of a scholar.... Scholarly research occurs when the facts and figures are

The Provost's Committee on University Outreach

transformed into new knowledge. Similarly, just as research is more than the gathering of information, so are teaching and outreach more than the transmission of facts. All three activities advance knowledge by the process which transforms information into understanding. Knowledge is based on but transcends information, and the transformation of information into new knowledge is the essence of scholarship.

And Boyer (1990:13) writes:

> We proceed with the conviction that if the nation's higher learning institutions are to meet today's urgent academic and social mandates, their missions must be carefully redefined and the meaning of scholarship creatively reconsidered.... "Redefining" (scholarship) means bringing to scholarship a broader meaning, one in which legitimacy is given to the full scope of academic work.

At Michigan State, applying Boyer's creative reconsideration of scholarship will require vigorous debate. That debate will include discussions about many issues, including how to evaluate the scholarly quality of outreach work, and how to separate outreach as scholarship vis-à-vis outreach that involves delivering knowledge in routine and repetitive ways.

Outreach as a Cross-Cutting Function

In the tripartite division of teaching, research, and service, outreach has been traditionally identified with "service." Outreach is better conceived as a cross-cutting function.

In the tripartite division of teaching, research, and service, outreach has been traditionally identified with "service." We suggest that outreach is better conceived as a **cross-cutting function.** In this way of thinking about outreach, there are forms of outreach teaching, research, and service, just as there are forms of non-outreach teaching, research, and service. For example, off-campus credit coursework is an example of outreach teaching. On-campus coursework offered for undergraduate students on Mondays-Fridays from 8 a.m.-5 p.m. represents non-outreach teaching. Collaborative, problem-solving research with external clientele is an example of outreach research, as contrasted with disciplinary research, which is often non-outreach research. And, medical and therapeutic services provided through a clinical service plan offers an example of outreach service. Service on university committees represents non-outreach service.

Some activities span categories and there are certainly linkages between non-outreach and outreach work.

Obviously, some activities span categories and there are certainly linkages between non-outreach and outreach work. For example, the results of non-outreach research are often later transmitted to users through outreach teaching and outreach service. There are also linkages across the teaching, research, and service categories. Technical assistance, for example, often spans teaching, research, and service. Technical assistance could be considered a form of teaching because it involves the transmission or communication of specialized knowledge. Yet it sometimes involves research. And a case could be made for thinking of it as a form of service. The important point is that technical assistance does constitute a form of outreach as long as it is scholarship conducted for the direct benefit of external audiences in ways that are consistent with University and unit missions.

Both types of linkages— between non-outreach and outreach activities, and between and among teaching, research, and service activities—are often required as Michigan State undertakes its activities.

Both types of linkages—between non-outreach and outreach activities, and between and among teaching, research, and service activities—are often required as Michigan

The Provost's Committee on University Outreach

These linkages add value to the efforts undertaken by MSU, and may also bring greater coherence to our lives as scholars.

State undertakes its activities. For example, an effort directed at improving the health of inner city young people might involve research pursued in collaboration with public and nonprofit agencies, seminars for education and health professionals, public policy consultation with elected city officials, guidance in the design and execution of large-scale murals by young people, and the joint organization of theatrical and musical events to clarify and dramatize key problems, and to raise funds to help address them.

These linkages add value to the efforts undertaken by MSU, and may also bring greater coherence to our lives as scholars. Indeed, many scholars organize and carry out their programs in exactly this way—sometimes without recognizing it, and at other times without receiving recognition from peers and administrators for integrating their scholarship across domains.

Service, Consulting, and Outreach

Just as is the case with teaching and research, there are outreach and non-outreach forms of service.

If outreach cuts across teaching, research, and service, how does this approach compare with the traditionally held view of outreach as service? Just as is the case with teaching and research, there are outreach and non-outreach forms of service.

As a form of outreach, service involves a scholar's efforts to generate, transmit, apply, or preserve knowledge for the direct benefit of external audiences in ways that are consistent with University and unit missions. Serving on a government commission, for example, is outreach service if the activity calls on the scholar's expertise and the subject-matter pertains to the programs and mission of the university unit(s) in which the scholar is appointed. On the other hand, if a chemist serves on the fundraising committee of a local nonprofit organization--a role that is apart from one's scholarly expertise and the programs of one's university unit--then that person engages in non-outreach service.

We do not exclude non-outreach service from the domain of outreach to diminish its importance. Indeed, this work is highly valued and often represents major contributions to society. It simply does not qualify as university outreach according to our definition.

Consulting requires scholarly expertise and frequently involves creating, transmitting, applying and/or preserving knowledge for the direct benefit of external audiences. But not all consulting is undertaken in conjunction with a unit's programs or advances a unit's mission.

Another important question is: How does our view of outreach apply to consulting? This is an important question because faculty and staff members routinely make knowledge available to the public, private, and nonprofit sectors in the form of consulting. This work is sometimes, but not always, undertaken on a fee-for-service basis.

Consulting requires scholarly expertise and frequently involves creating, transmitting, applying and/or preserving knowledge for the direct benefit of external audiences. But not all consulting is undertaken in conjunction with a unit's programs or advances a unit's mission. Consequently, it is our view that there is consulting-as-outreach and consulting-not-as-outreach. Whether a client pays a fee does not determine whether a consulting activity is outreach.

In making this distinction between two forms of consulting, we are not suggesting that all consulting efforts should be done as outreach. We only propose that there is an important distinction between the forms of consulting.

The Provost's Committee on University Outreach

The general principles outlined here can be drawn upon to create policies at the unit level so that it is clearly understood what constitutes outreach service and consulting-as-outreach. These policies are needed in order to address important issues such as faculty load and rewards.[3]

Outreach for the Direct Benefit of External Audiences

The University "reaches out" to external audiences in one or more of these dimensions: distance, time and place, and format and approach.

Through outreach, the University extends its knowledge resources for the direct benefit of external audiences. This includes such efforts as making it possible for students in distant locations to complete most of their degree programs without having to commute to the main campus, offering graduate courses on campus during the evening hours to better accommodate the schedules of working adults, providing noncredit instruction for professionals in new and important subject-matter, and collaborating on a research and development project with staff of a business or industry.

The University extends itself (or "reaches out") to external audiences in one or more of these dimensions: distance, time and place, and format and approach. It extends itself:

- in **distance** when it makes its knowledge resources accessible to those who do not live nearby;
- in **time** and **place** when knowledge resources are made available at convenient times and locations; and
- in **format** and **approach** when knowledge is made available in ways that are appropriate for those who seek it.

Outreach as a Major Feature of University and Unit Missions

Outreach should be considered a major function of the University, not a minor or ancillary function to be honored in rhetoric but minimized in practice.

As a land-grant university, Michigan State University has an historically recognized, as well as legislatively mandated, responsibility to extend its knowledge resources to the people of the state and the nation. Tradition, pragmatism, and University policy have made the reach of this responsibility global. MSU's outreach responsibilities and capacities are unique in the state. Accordingly, outreach should be considered a major function of the University, not a minor or ancillary function to be honored in rhetoric but minimized in practice.

Contributions of Outreach to the University

It seems obvious that the University contributes to the surrounding society through outreach, but it may be less obvious that outreach also makes three particularly important contributions to the University itself:

---

[3] A discussion of outreach as a cross-cutting form of scholarship may be found in the **Background Papers** report. Included in the discussion is a more extensive treatment of outreach and service, and consulting-as-outreach and consulting-not-as-outreach.

The Provost's Committee on University Outreach

Outreach affords faculty, staff, and students windows on current reality, and the perspectives gained through these windows inform a scholar's understanding of the contemporary meaning, value, and use of their disciplinary or professional knowledge.

Outreach creates an explicit link between the University and the larger society on which it depends for legitimacy and support.

Without the new and renewed knowledge generated by basic research, other forms of scholarship lose their base, their freshness, and their intellectual energy.

- **Vitality in Research and Teaching**

Outreach affords faculty, staff, and students windows on current reality, and the perspectives gained through these windows inform a scholar's understanding of the contemporary meaning, value, and use of their disciplinary or professional knowledge. Outreach also raises fascinating and important questions. As a result, on-campus research and teaching become more vital, more alive, and the intellectual life of the whole university is more stimulating.

- **Institutional Identity**

As both a land-grant and a research university, Michigan State has long represented a distinctive combination of teaching, research, and public service. Our definition of outreach changes the way these functions have traditionally been conceptualized and labeled. But in so doing, it highlights rather than diminishes the uniqueness of the University's identity among the state universities of Michigan. Even when outreach is restricted to solving problems with existing knowledge, it often inspires new research, thereby enriching and guiding the scholarly work of the university. Thus, outreach can exert a continuous shaping influence on the character, the orientation, and the activities of a university and its faculty, staff, and students.

- **Political and Financial Viability**

This identity, with the concomitant recognition of the University as a source of usable knowledge across many domains—social, scientific, technical, economic, educational, humanistic, medical, urban, and agricultural—has strong appeal for public, private, profit and nonprofit institutions, state and local governments, and individual citizens. Outreach also helps create an explicit link between the University and the larger society on which it depends for legitimacy and support.

Interdependence of Outreach and Other Functions

A robust program of basic research (i.e., non-outreach research) is crucial, not merely to the reputation of the University, but to its very ability to contribute to society. Without the new and renewed knowledge generated by basic research, other forms of scholarship lose their base, their freshness, and their intellectual energy.

Yet, basic research and other scholarship without obvious, direct application to current societal problems also profit from and *even depend upon* the public and political support that high-quality outreach engenders for the University. The contributions that the University makes to society through outreach are far more easily communicated to, and recognized by, the public and legislators, the governor, and other public representatives than are the subtler and more indirect contributions of basic research. Failure to grasp the dependence of basic research on outreach jeopardizes basic research. Such a failure is just as damaging to the cause of scholarship at MSU as is the failure to recognize the reciprocal dependence of outreach on basic research.

The Provost's Committee on University Outreach

Balance among the Functions

Even within our integrated way of thinking about outreach . . . the challenge of balancing these various activities remains.

Even within our integrated way of thinking about outreach, including the recognition that outreach and non-outreach activities overlap, influence, and contribute to each other, the challenge of balancing these various activities remains. Maintaining balance involves the thoughtful management of real and enduring tensions.

On the positive side, the fact that the university offers different types of knowledge-based services increases our adaptability. In difficult budget times, such as the present, if the demand for one of our services (e.g., undergraduate instruction) declines, another service can take up the slack. To take advantage of MSU's natural diversification, everyone in the University—the Board of Trustees and administration, as well as the faculty, staff, and students—must honor the full range of functions, supporting the different mixes of functions appropriate for different units at different points in time.

But there are important constituencies—internal as well as external—for all of our services (on-campus undergraduate and graduate instruction, formal and nonformal off-campus instruction, basic and applied research, and so on). At any given time, some of these constituencies will believe that the allocation of attention and resources among the services is out of balance.

To sustain the whole system as an institution with a land-grant mission, it is essential to maintain a working balance among the functions.

Because the several functions of the University are mutually dependent in the ways suggested above, they form a system. To sustain the whole system as an institution with a land-grant mission, it is essential to maintain a working balance among the functions. Paradoxically, if any function were to become dominant at the expense of the others then, in the long term, that function's very success might spell its own demise. For example, if on-campus undergraduate instruction were to consume too many resources at the expense of outreach, or outreach teaching were to use too many resources at the expense of basic research, then the *whole system*—including the temporarily ascendant function—would be jeopardized. The vitality of each function depends upon the vitality of all the others. Thus, the advocates for each function have a stake in the preservation of a working balance among the functions.

Just as we must begin to think much more in whole-system terms if humankind is to develop appropriately, we must also think much more in whole-system terms for the University to excel.

Broad comprehension of these systemic facts of life would moderate the inevitable tensions. Just as we must begin to think much more in whole-system terms if humankind is to develop appropriately, we must also think much more in whole-system terms for the University to excel. Some would argue that MSU could survive and even prosper with sharply reduced attention to both outreach and basic research, and a corresponding increase in attention to undergraduate instruction. We believe that, under such conditions, the institution that survived would no longer be Michigan State University as we know it.

Unfortunately, we do not know completely what the current level of outreach activity is or whether the balance of outreach and non-outreach activities is appropriate because, at present, MSU has a limited system for measuring many types of outreach activities. The creation of such a measurement system would facilitate more informed discussion of the appropriate balance.

Even so, there will be persistent and irreducible differences about the appropriate balance. There are significant differences even among members of the Outreach Committee. We all agree, however, that outreach should be a major function of the

The Provost's Committee on University Outreach

University, not a minor or ancillary function. Thus, our differences remain within a manageable range of tolerance. We believe that this is also true university-wide.

Finally, we also agree that the appropriate balance cannot be set by any one body for the entire university. Instead, the balance is and should be set through a dynamic process of discussion and negotiation at several levels: between university administrators and outside constituencies, between central administrators and deans, between deans and department chairs/school directors, and among chairs/directors, faculty members, and external constituents. This kind of dynamic interaction will enable the institution to adjust continually to changing circumstances and pressures without losing its equilibrium.

Outreach as an Integral Function

As a form of scholarship and a major function of the University, outreach should be integral to the intellectual life of the entire University, not isolated and marginalized in special units.

As a form of scholarship and a major function of the University, outreach should be integral to the intellectual life of the entire University, not isolated and marginalized in special units. At different levels and in ways appropriate to their discipline or profession, all academic units at MSU—though not necessarily every individual faculty member—should engage in outreach. For example, MSU Extension—as a major unit dedicated to outreach—can provide connections and support for faculty outreach activities. But MSUE cannot and should not be expected to take sole responsibility for outreach at Michigan State. To ensure a vital and energetic outreach mission, and for outreach to thrive at MSU, it must be a part of every academic unit.

Outreach and the Institutional Capacity to Adapt

The University is increasingly called upon to generate and provide knowledge about a widening array of social, cultural, economic, environmental, and technical challenges. The very pace of change in the society constantly creates new needs for knowledge and corollary needs for learning throughout the lifespan. A university in which outreach is integral to all units is in a far better position to respond to emerging problems and issues than one in which outreach is isolated in certain areas or units. Internal diversification enhances the institution's capacity to adapt to changing needs and circumstances.

Broadened Access

From the time of its founding in 1855, Michigan State University has provided access to postsecondary education for a much broader array of students than were served by traditional institutions of higher education. The University should continue to do so, but developments both within MSU and in the larger society suggest that the University's definition of "access" should itself be broadened.

Since MSU's founding, a dozen regional universities and many more community colleges have been launched and have matured into institutions serving every corner of the state. Together, they provide ready access to virtually anyone who wishes to pursue postsecondary education. Meanwhile, MSU has become a research university of national and international reputation, and the University has diversified

The Provost's Committee on University Outreach

and strengthened its capacities to extend the fruits of research to the people of the state, nation, and world.

At the same time, society has entered what many describe as a "knowledge age" with an emphasis on learning across the lifespan. Continuous learning is needed today by nearly everyone to maintain and improve one's standing in the job market, to exercise citizenship, to enhance the whole individual, to improve the business climate, and to fulfill a variety of other important sociocultural functions.

Given this dramatically transformed configuration of capacities across the state and within the University, and the advent of the knowledge age, MSU can and should provide access to knowledge through a wide array of outreach activities. MSU's approach to providing access to its knowledge resources must be responsive to societal needs with the overriding goal of maximizing the social and economic return on the state's public investment.

Setting the Outreach Agenda

Outreach activities should focus at the intersection of faculty expertise and interests, on the one hand, and high priority societal needs for knowledge, on the other. A close match between faculty expertise and the substantive foci of outreach activity is essential to ensure a robust level of authentically knowledge-based outreach, as well as to integrate outreach into the intellectual fabric of the university. Therefore, the problems, needs, and opportunities to be addressed through outreach should be chosen at levels close to the individual faculty member—the level of the department/school or multidisciplinary center and institute.

To ensure that outreach activities focus on important societal needs, however, all units will want to design thoughtful ways of identifying and setting priorities among problems, frequently through the direct participation of advisory groups representing key external constituencies along with formal needs assessments. Problems, needs, and opportunities are not objective facts but social and intellectual constructions. Ideally, the construction of needs and the setting of priorities are derived from discussion between faculty and external constituencies.

Because the needs of Michigan and the resulting demands for assistance from the University are practically limitless, setting priorities among needs inevitably proves far more difficult than identifying them. Outreach priorities will include problem-focused outreach as well as instructional outreach, including credit and noncredit instruction and professional continuing education.

University administrators can and should help units manage these expectations not only by providing assistance in designing unit- and college-level needs assessment and priority-setting systems, but also by conducting broad-gauged, statewide needs assessments and using the results to establish university-wide thematic priorities.

If expressed through the establishment of incentives for outreach related to the thematic priorities, leadership of this kind can enhance the coherence of the University's outreach agenda without unduly constraining unit-level decision making. Such coherence is crucial not only to effective outreach programming, but also to the

The Provost's Committee on University Outreach

MSU's approach to providing access to its knowledge resources must be responsive to societal needs with the overriding goal of maximizing the social and economic return on the state's public investment.

A close match between faculty expertise and the substantive foci of outreach activity is essential to ensure a robust level of authentically knowledge-based outreach, as well as to integrate outreach into the intellectual fabric of the university.

Because the needs of Michigan and the resulting demands for assistance from the University are practically limitless, setting priorities among needs inevitably proves far more difficult than identifying them.

An integrated, decentralized approach to priority setting allows each unit considerable flexibility to set an agenda that will enable its faculty to make the maximum contribution.

University's ability to tell its story effectively to the public, the legislature, the governor, and specific constituencies around the state, nation, and world.

Productivity and Accountability

The mix of activities pursued by a unit will depend upon such factors as the nature of the discipline, field, or profession to which it relates, the levels of seniority and range of talents represented in its faculty, and the demands and opportunities for non-outreach activity (e.g., for on-campus instruction and externally funded basic research), as well as the demands and opportunities for outreach activity. An integrated, decentralized approach to priority setting allows each unit considerable flexibility to set an agenda that will enable its faculty to make the maximum contribution.

With this flexibility goes a responsibility to honor the full range of the University's mission, including the proposition that outreach is a major function that cannot be neglected by any academic unit.

With this flexibility goes a responsibility to honor the full range of the University's mission, including the proposition that outreach is a major function that cannot be neglected by any academic unit. A unit should deliberately choose a mix of activities that enables all of its members to contribute the maximum to the total scholarly productivity of the unit, and outreach as conceptualized here provides units with a broadened array of ways to demonstrate productivity.

Multidisciplinary Centers/ Institutes And Outreach

Because of their complexity, many problems in contemporary society can only be understood with the aid of theories, concepts, and methods from multiple disciplines. Just as multidisciplinary centers have proven essential organizational vehicles for much basic research and on-campus instruction, they also hold considerable value for integrating outreach research, teaching, and service.

These centers and institutes offer a convenient way to bring to bear knowledge from across the University. They may also represent an increasingly important organizational form as the University moves into the twenty-first century.

If the concept of outreach as a major, connected, integral, knowledge-based form of scholarship is to become a reality at MSU, the University must stimulate, support, and reward outreach appropriately.

Stimulating, Supporting, and Rewarding Outreach

If the concept of outreach as a major, connected, integral, knowledge-based form of scholarship is to become a reality at MSU, the University must stimulate, support, and reward outreach appropriately. That is, we must find ways to make outreach—

- intrinsically appealing by providing opportunities for the expression of authentic faculty interests through outreach;
- no more burdensome than non-outreach activities by offering effective forms of administrative and technological support; and
- well-rewarded through incentive and recognition programs, as well as more prominence in evaluation, promotion, and tenure processes.

The Provost's Committee on University Outreach

Measures to make outreach attractive are far more likely to weave outreach into the fabric of the University than are hard-nosed pressures and penalties.

The Challenge

American universities are facing a major challenge to maintain quality and be more responsive to the needs of society. University outreach activities do play and must continue to play a major role in meeting this challenge. Michigan State University, as both a land-grant and a major research university, has long maintained a commitment to all components of scholarly activity: knowledge generation, transmission, application, and preservation. By broadening its view of outreach and integrating that view more completely into the structure and function of the University, MSU is in a unique position to provide the kinds of outreach activities that will respond to society's needs while maintaining excellence in all knowledge domains.

Even when the expertise exists within the University to address a number of societal problems, however, human resources, time, money and personnel will fall short of demand; the needs of society far exceed the ability of the University to respond. Therefore, responding to outreach demands will require setting priorities and carefully managing available resources.

The defining dimensions of outreach just described, and the strategic directions for strengthening outreach that follow, are this committee's attempt to provide a framework for guiding the development of priorities related to Michigan State University's outreach response.

Michigan State University, as both a land-grant and a major research university, has long maintained a commitment to all components of scholarly activity: knowledge generation, transmission, application, and preservation.

The Provost's Committee on University Outreach

Excerpt from:

REPORT OF THE UNIVERSITY OF NORTH CAROLINA AT CHAPEL HILL PUBLIC SERVICE ROUNDTABLE

II. FINDINGS AND RECOMMENDATIONS

1. *Public service is a complex concept which is best understood as embracing several distinctive types of contributions to the state, its citizens, and the world at large.*

The Roundtable as a whole, and each of its subcommittees, concluded that the phrase "public service" is not self-defining, and that, indeed, this phrase appears to mean a variety of different things within diverse academic disciplines, and among varied external constituencies. At its first plenary meeting of 1993-94, members of the Roundtable shared individual opinions on the meaning of public service. During the fall semester, the co-chairs of the Roundtable informally disseminated a "public service inventory" questionnaire to a variety of contacts across the campus, in order to develop a better understanding of how various units and faculty members described (and thus defined) their own public service activities.

Finally, the co-chairs, as well as the SACS reaccreditation task force working in the area of public service, gathered information about definitions of public service from other campuses (including such schools as Minnesota, Michigan State, Georgia, Illinois, North Carolina State, and the Association of Land-Grant Colleges), several different professional organizations, and various aspects of the UNC system. Some of these sources tended to use the term "outreach" instead of "public service," particularly in instances in which the institution had traditionally provided agricultural extension services.

During the Roundtable's ongoing discussions of the meaning of public service, several points became clear. The Roundtable determined that it is critical to adopt a shared "conceptual framework" or "working definition" to guide and focus the ongoing discussions of public service on this campus over the next one to two years. That conceptual framework, or working definition should reflect a number of key assumptions:

▶ "Public service" should not be so broadly defined that every undertaking associated with the university falls within its ambit. Moreover, community service by individual faculty, staff or students in their role as private citizens (such as jury duty, youth coaching, the PTA, etc.) is private service and not university public service.

▶ "Public service" as a concept is broader than the narrow definition of "institutional service" sometimes used in academic settings to refer to departmental committee work or other similar functions.

▶ "Public service" in its truest sense is a concept that can inform, transcend, and cut across all three of the basic components of the university's traditional mission statement (research, teaching, and service).

▶ "Public service" activities within the university share a number of key characteristics, including contribution to the public welfare or the common good; reliance on the professional or academic expertise of university faculty, staff or students; and response to practical problems, issues, interests or concerns of our society.

▶ "Public service" activities within the university may also vary in a number of respects. They may occur on or off campus; may in some cases be compensated (although activities engaged in mainly to make money are clearly not university public service, may benefit a variety of individuals including members of the public, local, state, national and international governing bodies and agencies.

▶ "Public service" for present purposes can best be understood as encompassing several illustrative types of activities. These categories should not be seen as exclusive, and additional categories and illustrations will undoubtedly continue to be added as the university community more fully explores the meaning of "public service."

▶ The conceptual framework or working definition of "public service" set forth in this report should not be seen as a final or definitive framework or definition. Instead, it should provide a basis for intensive discussions of the meaning of public service within the campus community until we are sure that a consensus definition had been fully considered and embraced. We are hopeful that this continuing conversation will also allow us to work with nearby universities and others within the UNC System to develop a shared understanding of the meaning of "public service" in order to foster more effective cooperation and coordination of our efforts on behalf of the state.

a. We accordingly recommend that the conceptual framework or working definition of "public service" developed by the Roundtable and refined in connection with the UNC-CH SACS self-study of public service activities, continue to be used as the focus of our work in the coming one to two years. That working definition is set forth in full at appendix B, and can be briefly summarized as follows:

"Public service" activities generally fall into the following categories: (A) continuing education; (B) lifelong learning opportunities; (C) access to library, educational facilities, and cultural resources; (D) direct services, especially for members of the public with limited financial resources; (E) action-oriented teaching in the form of clinical education, service internships or practica; (F) action-oriented research focused on responding to vexing public problems; (G) research dissemination and consultation which shares professional expertise, technology, and evaluation capabilities; and (H) leadership which keeps higher education in North Carolina at the cutting edge or otherwise benefits society. □

Excerpt from:

APPOINTMENTS, PROMOTION, AND TENURE MANUAL

School of Public Health, University of North Carolina at Chapel Hill
Adopted October 1, 1994

V. SPECIFIC CRITERIA FOR APPOINTMENTS AND PROMOTIONS

C. PUBLIC HEALTH PRACTICE

As presently construed, for the purposes of promotion and tenure, public health practice has the following connotations:

▶ a faculty member works with a national, state, or local health agency, or directly with a community, to help solve some current public health problem;

▶ or a faculty member works in another setting, e.g., international, health care, or worksite;

▶ often the role of the faculty member is one of collaboration with health agencies and communities, rather that the more traditional role of "principal investigator;"

▶ the results of the work are directly and immediately applicable, as compared to the more "distant" application of research findings;

▶ practice usually involves helping health agencies assess public health problems or, plan, implement or evaluate public health programs;

▶ practice often involves helping communities or health agencies assess public health problems, assure the delivery of public health services, or develop public health policies;

▶ practice often involves the faculty member in direct contact with communities or populations that are the clients, recipients or beneficiaries of public health programs or services;

▶ the program planning, implementing and evaluating process is often long-term and time intensive;

▶ the "scholarly" product of practice is in the form of technical reports, presentations to professional meetings, and/or "program" type publications in the more traditional research journals;

▶ practice often has an advocacy component;

▶ there is a linkage between a faculty member's practice experiences and the teaching of public health graduate students; such linkage may be in the classroom or it may be in supervised field experiences, or other similar types of experiences in which graduate students work with or under the supervision of the practice faculty member;

▶ there can be a research component to practice: practice oriented research is defined by communities/agencies and deals with immediate problems; the practitioner/ researcher collaborates with communities/agencies, and the research is jointly owned;

▶ there can be a service component to practice: practice oriented service is community and/or health agency based, is long-term, and helps communities and/or agencies define, and/or solve immediate public health problems.

For promotion and tenure purposes, public health practice must be deemed to be "scholarly." That is, the practice must be shown to have effected not only a given policy, community, agency or program, but it must also be shown that the practice has in some way contributed to advancing the state-of-the-art of public health practice itself.

Evidence of accomplishment in public health practice should be provided for one or more major projects. As rank increases, it is expected that both the quantity and quality of practice will also increase.

Competence in public health practice can be demonstrated by providing the following types of materials and information at time of promotion and tenure:

1. Description of public health practice activities.
2. For each practice project, the nature and duration of the project, and the role played by the faculty member.
3. Documentation that the practice contributions have had important effects on policy, and/or on a community, agency or program.
4. Evidence that the practice activities involved or resulted in the creation or development of new public health or similar systems for the improvement of the publics' health.
5. Evidence that the public health practice activities have contributed to the teaching activities of the faculty member and/or the department; for instance, that teaching is directed at practice issues such as assessing public health problems, assuring the delivery of public health services, or developing public health policies.
6. Evidence that teaching contributions include linking classroom activities and other teaching activities with public health agencies.
7. Evidence that new knowledge, methods, or policies derived from the candidate's public health practice have diffused to other communities, or health agencies.

8. Evidence that new practice ideas, policies, programs, methods, etc. have been disseminated through publications. In addition to articles in refereed journals, "publication" can mean producing technical reports that are used by public health agencies and/or communities to help them assess public health problems, assure the delivery of public health services, or develop public health policies.

   The equivalent of peer review of such technical reports is evidence of their impact (e.g. letters indicating that a technical report was used to help assess public health problems, assure the delivery of public health services, or develop public health policies). The impact of technical reports should also be documented by independent reviewers.

9. Receiving honors or awards in recognition of outstanding contributions to public health practice.

10. Invitations by other institutions or health agencies to help plan, organize or review public health practice activities.

11. Appointments to national commissions, committees, boards, etc. related to public health practice.

12. Grants and contracts received to fund public health practice activities. □

A Faculty Guide for Relating Public Service to the Promotion and Tenure Review Process

University of Illinois at Urbana-Champaign

This guide was written by James A. Farmer, Jr., and Steven F. Schomberg in cooperation with the members of the Senate Committee for Continuing Education and Public Service, 1990-93. Material was drawn from a study of faculty views about public service conducted in 1991.

The results of the study are more fully discussed by Steven F. Schomberg and James A. Farmer, Jr., in "The Evolving Concept of Public Service and Implications for Rewarding Faculty," *Continuing Higher Education Review,* Vol. 58, no. 3, Fall 1994.

A FACULTY GUIDE FOR RELATING PUBLIC SERVICE TO THE PROMOTION AND TENURE REVIEW PROCESS[1]

PURPOSE OF THIS GUIDE

This guide was prepared by the Senate Committee on Continuing Education and Public Service and the Office of Continuing Education and Public Service. It should be used by faculty members whose public service responsibilities are major or minor components of their duties. Department heads also will find the guidelines helpful as they advise faculty members on the preparation of materials for promotion and tenure review.

The guide is in two parts. In the first part, public service is described, examples of public service activities are presented, and potential sources of confusion about public service are identified and discussed. In the second part, suggestions are made for planning, documenting, and evaluating public service.

PART I
DEFINING THE SCOPE OF PUBLIC SERVICE

The campus guidelines for promotion and tenure issued by the Office of the Vice Chancellor for Academic Affairs make it clear that:

The three prime missions of the University are teaching, research, and public service. In any promotion process, consideration should be given to performance of the individual in all three of these areas. However, the three should not be treated equally and their application depends upon the definition of the position to which the individual has been appointed and to which he or she is to be promoted. (1992-93 Academic Affairs Communication No. 9)

This guide focuses on public service and also discusses how public service interacts with teaching and research. Much as the research (scholarship) of individuals may positively affect their teaching and public service, so too their involvement in public service may

---

1. This guide replaces a previous one prepared jointly by the University Senate and the Office of Continuing Education and Public Service in the late 1970s. Ideas were also drawn from the literature on assessment and from the guidelines used by the University of California System; the University of California, Davis; the University of Wisconsin; Michigan State University; and the University of Georgia.

Internet users may print this publication for reference use. To access the complete document on Gopher go to: University of Illinois at Urbana-Champaign/Other Gopher and Information Servers/Continuing Education and Public Service. A limited number of copies of this guide are available from the Office of Continuing Education and Public Service at the University of Illinois at Urbana-Champaign. Requests for copies may be sent to strader@ux1.cso.uiuc.edu. Please include your name, title, and mailing address.

positively serve the purposes of their research and teaching. Such is the case for clinical teaching, where public service and teaching are closely integrated. Public service opportunities may evolve from research projects in fields such as agriculture, business, education, and engineering; in response to external requests; or from needs analyses. Public service may lead to subsequent research activities. This interaction among teaching, research, and public service can contribute significantly to the vitality of the institution, its colleges, units, and departments, as well as to the vitality of its individual faculty members.

Distinguishing Characteristics of Activities Considered as Public Service

The types of public service activities that faculty members engage in reflect the nature of their appointments, their training and experience, as well as specific external needs. This leads to diverse forms of interaction by faculty members with communities, individual clients, industries, agencies, governmental entities, and other constituencies. Although the forms can be diverse, public service activities share the following three distinguishing characteristics:

1. They contribute to the public welfare or the common good.
2. They call upon faculty members' academic and/or professional expertise.
3. They directly address or respond to real-world problems, issues, interests, or concerns.

The first characteristic signifies the importance of determining the purpose of a particular activity. Doing so can help avoid confusing public service activities that are for the common good and those that are primarily of only private interest and benefit. The second characteristic emphasizes the importance of differentiating volunteer community activities, such as that of a professor coaching youth league softball, from activities that require the professional expertise of the professor. The final characteristic reflects a weighting toward applied activities rather than theoretical ones on the perceived continuum between theory and practice. Public service activities tend to focus primarily on the concrete rather than on the abstract.

Examples of Public Service Activities

The diversity of external needs as well as faculty training and experience leads to many different forms of public service. To the extent that they are in keeping with all three of the previously stated characteristics, the following activities are examples of how faculty members, through their academic or professional expertise, can contribute to the public good while directly addressing real-world problems, issues, interests, or concerns:

▶ Provide services for the public through a University clinic, hospital, or laboratory.

▶ Make research understandable and usable in specific professional and applied settings such as in technology transfer activities.

▶ Provide public policy analysis for local, state, national, or international governmental agencies.

▶ Test concepts and processes in real-world situations.

▶ Act as expert witnesses.

▶ Give presentations or performances for the public.

▶ Provide extension education.

▶ Conduct applied research.

▶ Evaluate programs, policies, or personnel for agencies.

▶ Engage in informational activities (seminars, conferences, institutes) that address public-interest problems, issues, and concerns and that are aimed at either general or specialized audiences such as commodity, trade, practitioner or occupational groups.

▶ Participate in governmental meetings or on federal review panels.

▶ Engage in economic and community development activities.

▶ Participate in collaborative endeavors with schools, industry, or civic agencies.

▶ Testify before legislative or congressional committees.

▶ Consult with town, city, or county governments; schools, museums, parks, and other public institutions; companies; groups; or individuals.

▶ Assist neighborhood organizations.

▶ Conduct studies on specific problems brought to one's attention by individuals, agencies, or businesses.

▶ Serve as experts for the press or other media.

▶ Write for popular and nonacademic publications, including newsletters and magazines directed to agencies, professionals, or other specialized audiences.

Such activities usually require (1) a background of significant scholarship, (2) adequate diagnostic skills, (3) use or development of creative and focused methodologies, (4) strong information organization and media skills, and (5) written and oral skills in interpreting as well as presenting information.

Potential Sources of Confusion

1. Public service may be performed in many different locations: on campus, as when serving in a clinic or hospital; or off campus, as when consulting with a school district or a governmental agency. *Location,* therefore, is not a distinguishing characteristic of public service.

2. Public service typically entails the application of faculty members' areas of expertise in addressing real-world problems, issues, or concerns. Such service may be performed as part of their University responsibilities or in addition to their stated responsibilities, in which case it may be either uncompensated or compensated. In terms of compensation, the nature and extent of all public service work should be in keeping with University regulations. Whether or not *compensation* is received for public service is not a criterion for an activity's being considered public service. At the same time, activities that are engaged in mainly to make money, such as running a business or a consulting firm on the side, are clearly not part of faculty members' University public service activities, even though those activities may benefit the public, organizations, or individuals.

3. *Recipients* of public service may include individuals and organizations, as well as local, state, national, and international governing bodies and agencies. Activities directed primarily to regularly enrolled students would not normally be considered public service. While it is certainly a form of service to individuals and the state, teaching regularly enrolled students in this University, no matter where their instruction takes place, would normally be considered a form of instruction in promotion and tenure considerations.

4. *Clinical teaching* is clearly a blend of teaching and public service. Although arising from a primary teaching need, the primary obligation during its performance is to patients or clients, and only secondarily to the students. The welfare of the patients or clients must be kept foremost. Experimentation solely for instructional purpose would be unethical.

5. Not all forms of service are *public* service. For example, faculty members can provide service to the University: in an administrative capacity; as members of the senate; or as committee members at the University, campus, college, or departmental levels. Such service, however, is not public service and is referred to as **institutional service** or **internal service**; nor is service to professional organizations and scholarly societies, which is typically referred to as **disciplinary service.**

6. Not all activities engaged in by faculty members in settings external to the University are undertaken to help fulfill the university's or unit's public service mission. (College, unit, and departmental mission statements are important in this regard because the institution's mission is too broad to offer much guidance on this matter.) For example, faculty members may serve as jurors, as youth leaders and coaches, or on the PTA. They do so, however, in their role as private citizens. Therefore, such service is sometimes

referred to as **private service.** In contrast, **public service** activities fulfill the mission of the unit and institution and utilize faculty members' academic or professional expertise.

7. The relationships among outreach, continuing education, and public service are potentially confusing. Both public service and continuing education are forms of *outreach* when they go beyond resident instruction and discipline-oriented research and are initiated in response to an external audience or constituency. However, the outreach concept often does not describe the reciprocal nature of the interaction between faculty members and their publics. For example, while faculty members are working with external audiences, they often gain insight into problems and receive knowledge that affects their research and informs their teaching.

    Some but not all types of *public service* are accomplished through *continuing education* such as community short courses and continuing professional education. However, some types of continuing education primarily serve the University's teaching mission, such as when graduate programs are offered at off-campus sites. Continuing education that does meet all three of the previously stated characteristics of public service serves the University's public service mission, while continuing education that does not meet all three of the above criteria primarily serves the teaching mission.

8. Consulting with private companies can be an important form of public service, and interaction with companies can contribute to faculty members' research (scholarship) and/or teaching. To be considered part of one's University public service, consulting should conform to all three of the above criteria of public service and reflect the department's and University's mission objectives. At the same time, the main purpose of consulting should be service rather than financial remuneration.

9. Public service is a complex set of activities reflecting the nature of faculty members' appointments, their training and experience as well as the specific external need. Sometimes, *differentiating these activities from teaching and research* is difficult, and in such cases multiple criteria should be used in assessing the quality of the activity. However, for the activity to be public service it must draw upon faculty members' academic or professional expertise and contribute to the public good, while at the same time directly addressing or responding to real-world problems, issues, interests, or concerns.

PART II
SUGGESTIONS FOR PLANNING, DOCUMENTING, AND EVALUATING PUBLIC SERVICE

This guide emphasizes the importance of planning early, understanding departmental expectations, designing activities with evaluation in mind, and being sure that any evaluation is consistent with the demands of the promotion and tenure review process. Far too often, faculty members who make an impact through their public service activities fail to receive appropriate recognition because they and their department heads did not pay proper attention to one or more of these considerations.

The first part of this section is intended for all faculty members who perform public service work, regardless of the emphasis placed upon it. However, the final section is addressed specifically to those faculty members whose public service responsibilities constitute a substantial portion of their University-assigned responsibilities.

Recommendations for All Faculty Members

All faculty members will benefit from the following suggestions for planning, documenting, and evaluating public service.

Understanding the institution

The University of Illinois at Urbana-Champaign is a **land-grant** and **research-intensive** institution. Therefore, the general criteria applied to the judgment of merit reflect an expectation for excellence in teaching, research, and public service. The specific expectations are reviewed annually and communicated to the colleges by the Office of the Vice Chancellor for Academic Affairs.

Understanding unit or departmental expectations

The promotion and tenure process begins with the specific academic department or unit; therefore, faculty members' involvement in public service should reflect their position appointments. Departments vary in the emphasis they give to public service activities and those they consider important. Discussions with the department head or chair, other senior members of the department's faculty, and members of the department's promotion and tenure review committee can help to clarify the following:

1. Departmental expectations concerning the kinds of public service activities that are encouraged
2. How each activity should be documented

3.   The criteria for public service to be used in judging performance at the departmental and college level.

Questions to be considered:

▶   In what areas has the department established a history of quality in public service?

▶   In what ways do the department's faculty members appropriately interact with practicing professionals or meet agency and industry needs for technical information and education?

▶   What types of public service activities are encouraged as a part of the departmental mission?

▶   Does the faculty member's position appointment fit within the mission of the department and/or college?

▶   What balance does the department expect faculty members to maintain among research (or other scholarly activities), teaching (including continuing education), and public service while working toward indefinite tenure?

It is important to establish a dialogue at the appropriate level(s) of the University regarding expectations for professional development and productivity. Dialogues of this type should continue throughout faculty members' careers.

Preparing early for evaluation

Preparing for evaluation of public service work by promotion and tenure committees should begin early in a faculty member's University appointment. As public service activities are planned, conducted, and evaluated, consider how those activities might best be interpreted to promotion or tenure committees. Developing high-quality public service activities takes time and effort. Thoughtful evaluation and reporting of evaluation results also require time and effort. Beginning early will help to avoid a last-minute rush to document work and should result in a clearer and more complete interpretation of accomplishments.

Seeking help

Many sources of assistance are available to faculty members as they plan, conduct, evaluate, and report their public service work. Faculty members should seek out a mentor and advocate among the senior faculty members. Many committees do not have experience with evaluating public service activities; a senior faculty member who understands the public service concept and how to organize a dossier can help a committee evaluate these activities and understand how they fit into the portfolio.

Planning public service with promotion in mind

If public service activities are to be used to support a favorable promotion decision, they should be planned with that use in mind. Faculty members should plan their efforts far in advance and design them for qualitative evaluation. Department chairs or heads should be involved in the planning process to ensure that faculty members' proposed public service activities are consistent with departmental expectations. Departmental executive committee members, senior faculty members, and promotion and tenure committee members should also be asked to share their insights regarding the campus promotion process.

Planning activities with evaluation in mind

As faculty members become involved in public service, evaluation should be included as part of the planning of any such activity. The best way to assure that public service efforts will be assessed at the end of an activity is to develop evaluative mechanisms that will track those efforts from the beginning.

Assessment can be helpful both to improve work along the way and to determine its quality at the end of an activity. These two types of evaluations should be performed separately. Evaluation of quality should consider the kinds of evidence and the outcomes that will be meaningful to promotion and tenure committee members at the departmental, college, and campus levels. *Simply listing activities without attention to assessment of quality does little to enhance a case for promotion or tenure.* Assessment of quality should include evidence of excellence, innovation, and impact. Faculty members should be able to identify relevant evaluative criteria and check their judgment against that of colleagues.

Public service needs to be visible, evaluatable, and improvable. Public service activities typically occur outside the view of other faculty members. Therefore, it is important that tangible products result from public service activities and that they can be evaluated by others. Writing up public service as a form of scholarship is one way to permit evaluation of the work.

Making a case

Make a case for the quality of the public service work and how it relates to research and/or teaching. Relate the case explicitly to the terms of the appointment with the University. Promotion and tenure committees judge how well the case has been made either for the granting of indefinite tenure or promotion. They do not evaluate the specific work itself; this is done by the external referees. Therefore, it is not the quality of any one piece of work but the overall quality of the dossier and the accompanying documentation that will lead to a successful outcome.

Being selective

Not everything undertaken as a public service will be or should be considered in promotion and tenure review. For example, routine talks to service clubs or repeated consultation on the same topic with similar information may not be considered as significant for review. Consider the following questions as a way of relating public service activities to the promotion and tenure process:

▶   Do the public service efforts draw upon the faculty member's disciplinary or professional expertise?

▶   To what extent do the activities represent potential new interpretations and applications of knowledge for use in specific settings?

▶   Is there potential for the activities to generate new research questions or make more understandable the current body of knowledge?

▶   Does the outreach activity make an impact on public policy, on the improvement of practice among professionals, or on those involved in agriculture or business?

▶   Is there continuity among program ideas, or do they present a "shotgun" array of activities?

Making quality evident

Participants in public service activities conducted by University faculty members are often active professionals in various fields. They are in an appropriate position to assess the impact of such activities when the primary focus is on applying current knowledge to practical problems. They may also be able to provide evidence of the contribution of scholarly endeavors to any increase of their awareness of the practical implications of theory or to any improvement of professional practice. In summary, documentation of the impact of public service activities and their contributions to professional improvement may be the most potent single manner in which comments by professionals can support the case in the review process.

Senior faculty members from comparable institutions represent a valuable source of evidence regarding the excellence of faculty members' public service efforts and related scholarly endeavors. In particular, they may be able to comment on the extent to which faculty members have made a substantial contribution to their discipline or profession and the extent to which they have been recognized by other scholars, public policy makers, or practitioners.

The qualifications of referees asked to comment upon leadership in the field or contributions to theory through public service efforts *must* be made explicit in promotion papers. Although faculty members from comparable institutions are preferred, it is imperative that review committee members be able to identify why the particular referees are to be viewed as highly qualified to assess the faculty member's standing. Referees' comments should be specific and concise. The context in which the faculty member is being judged and the evaluator's qualifications and background are all critical to the ultimate impact of the reference. The more familiar the referees are with the particular public service effort, similar efforts, and the field in general and the more focused their evaluative comments, the more helpful will be their evaluations.

Recommendations for Faculty Members Whose Public Service Constitutes a Substantial Portion of Their University-Assigned Responsibilities

Faculty members whose University-assigned responsibilities entail a significant amount of public service work are strongly urged to develop with the department head or chair and the dean at the time of hiring any *special criteria* for judging the quality of public service activities to be used in evaluating the quality of performance. Such criteria should then be made available to candidates in writing at the time of their appointment. Subsequent modifications in official appointment papers should likewise be documented and become part of their official personnel records.

Special criteria for judging public service

When special criteria are being negotiated, the following topics related to how they will be evidenced in the final portfolio should be covered:

1. Quality of public service work
2. Impact of the public service work
3. Dissemination of the public service contribution as expressed through scholarship
4. Interaction with a community of scholars
5. Integration of research (scholarship), teaching, and public service

For purposes of promotion and tenure decisions, well-stated cases should be based on the overall public service activities, not on a single instance of public service. Faculty members will want to stress the nature and extent of interaction with society. Most committees will encourage that only those public service activities that are exemplary and can clearly demonstrate impact and innovation be put forward. Well-stated cases will also argue effectively how the efforts to bridge between theory and real-world problems, issues, or concerns have not only enhanced faculty members' careers, but have also contributed to the vitality of the University and larger community.

Long lists of public service activities do not necessarily indicate anything about the quality of those activities. Indeed, high-quality activities may be obscured or invisible when buried in a lengthy list of unevaluated activities. Only the best efforts should be included in the dossier. The activity should be described briefly, along with its impact and outcomes, the evaluation procedures used, the context in which comparisons were made, and the qualifications of evaluators.

It is advisable to contact relevant professional and discipline-oriented associations and societies to obtain their statements, if available, about specific criteria for evaluating public service in their fields.

Public service is generally regarded of high quality when there is evidence that it has resulted in the following outcomes:

▶ A beneficial impact attributable at least in part to the application of relevant and up-to-date knowledge to the real-world problems, issues, or concerns addressed by the public service (Examples: favorable effects upon public policy or upon professional, agricultural, or business practice)

▶ Honors, awards, and other forms of special recognition such as commendations that have been received in the execution of public service

▶ Election to office or undertaking important service to professional associations and learning societies, including editorial work or peer reviewing for a national or international organization, as related to public service

▶ Selection for special public service activities outside the state and invitations to give talks within the faculty member's field

▶ Election or appointment to departmental or institutional governance bodies or to academic policy or procedure development committees related to public service

▶ Participation in professional or scientific associations and meetings, and presentation of papers

Evidence of scholarly excellence

Tenure-track and tenured faculty members whose main responsibility is providing public service are generally expected to engage in scholarly endeavors that result in innovations, advancement in knowledge, or contributions to their disciplines or professions in their service to society. Efforts to improve public service can be a form of scholarly activity related to research and can result in publication. In addition, public service that is truly innovative can advance a discipline or profession and attract external support. Evidence of scholarly excellence in these endeavors may include:

▶ Publication in books, journals, and monographs; creation of videotapes, computer programs, and fact sheets; syllabus reprints; development of program materials; authored newspaper articles; exhibits, shows, and concerts; writing for business, trade, and community publications and technical reports. (In such publications, for example, the results of innovative links made between theory and practice may be described.)

▶ Evaluative statements from clients or peers of quality and impact of reports and other documents produced by the faculty member that evidence creativity and scholarship in public service.

▶ Receiving grants and contracts to fund the development and delivery of public service innovations, when such grants and contracts are competitive and subject to peer review and approval.

▶ Being sought out by individuals from outside the state or nation who want to study the public service provider's work and innovations.

▶ Development of instruments and processes adopted by others for solving persistent problems.

SUMMARY

Public service work is an important part of the mission of the University of Illinois at Urbana-Champaign. However, its form of expression is influenced by a faculty member's particular department and college. Engaging in public service activities is a role all faculty members can and should perform from time to time, but the importance of doing so tends to vary by the different stages of an individual's academic career.

The first part of this guide describes the diversity of public service opportunities and clarifies some of the confusion that can arise in their evaluation relative to promotion and tenure considerations. The second part of the guide provides important information regarding how to make a case that an individual's performance is of high quality, that it is integrated with teaching and research (scholarship), and that it makes an impact on the quality of life. Use of this guide by faculty members, department heads, and committees should lead to better-supported promotion and tenure documents, more successful cases, and more fulfilled and appropriately rewarded faculty members.   □